MYTH AND MANKIND

Lost Realms of Gold

SOUTH AMERICAN MYTH

MYTH AND MANKIND

LOST REALMS OF GOLD: South American Myth
Writers: Tony Allan (Kingdoms of Gold, Empire of the Sun, The Amerindian Legacy), Clifford Bishop (After the Conquest, The Forest People), Charles Phillips (Realm of the Condor)
Consultant: Andrew Canessa

Created, edited and designed by
Duncan Baird Publishers
Castle House
75–76 Wells Street
London W1P 3RE

DUNCAN BAIRD PUBLISHERS
Managing Editor: Diana Loxley
Managing Art Editor: Gabriella Le Grazie

Series Editor: Christina Rodenbeck
Editors: Mark McDowall, Lucy Rix
Designer: Christine Keilty
Picture Researcher: Cecilia Weston-Baker
Artworks: Neil Gower
Map Artworks: Lorraine Harrison
Artwork Borders: Iona McGlashan

TIME-LIFE BOOKS
Staff for LOST REALMS OF GOLD:
South American Myth

Editorial Manager: Tony Allan
Design Consultant: Mary Staples
Editorial Production: Justina Cox

Published by Time-Life Books BV, Amsterdam
First Time-Life English language printing 1998
TIME-LIFE is a trademark of
Time Warner Inc, USA

ISBN 0 7054 3583 0

Colour separation by Colourscan, Singapore
Printed and bound by Milanostampa, SpA, Farigliano, Italy

Title page: **This vessel is decorated with a hunter clutching his catch, and dates from *c.*AD100.**

Contents page: **A fantastic grinning figure cavorts on this Paracas culture textile, dated *c.*500BC.**

30 29 28 27 26 25 24 23 22 21 20 19 18 17 16 15 14 13 12 11 10 9 8 7 6 5 4 3 2 1

Contents

KINGDOMS OF GOLD

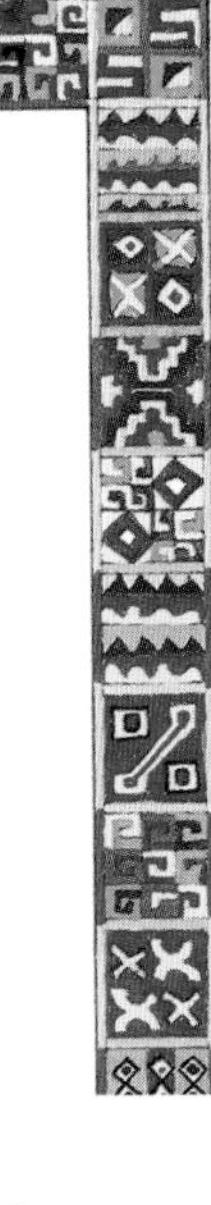

One morning in 1527, the inhabitants of the Inca city of Tumbes on the Peruvian coast were astonished to see a mysterious ship sailing into harbour. Aboard were a handful of battle-hardened adventurers of a race that seemed quite as strange and foreign as the white-sailed barque they manned. In fact they were Spanish conquistadors under the leadership of the 49-year-old Francisco Pizarro. With their arrival, contact between South America's greatest indigenous civilization and the rest of the world was firmly secured, with results that quickly proved calamitous for the native peoples.

Pizarro and his men were made welcome and invited to tour the city. What they saw amazed them: marvellously-engineered aqueducts, a fortress whose walls were built of vast blocks of unmortared stone, and, most impressive of all, a temple clad with plates of gold and silver. In its garden were the most luscious fruit and vegetables – all made of precious metals.

That gold was to prove the Indians' undoing. Driven on by the prospect of unlimited riches, Pizarro returned five years later with an army that quickly made itself master of the entire Inca empire. Within twenty years of his arrival most of the continent was under Spanish or Portuguese control.

The European takeover almost sounded the death knell of a culture that had evolved over more than 10,000 years. The native gods were branded delusions of Satan, and traditional beliefs and customs were proscribed as the Spanish sought to spread their Christian faith throughout the newly-claimed continent. The Indians watched passively while their temples were torn down and their sacred images destroyed.

Yet something of their heritage survived the great cataclysm. Churchmen sympathetic to their plight wrote down details of the native peoples' old beliefs. Among the converts, traditional customs often survived under a Christian veneer. And in the continent's remoter areas people continued to follow their traditional ways undisturbed. Here the tribes resisted conquest since their social systems were less top-heavy than that of the Incas, and did not necessarily collapse when their leader was killed. And to this rich seam of native lore the Spanish conquest even added legends of its own – of golden El Dorados, of giants, Amazons and other wonders of a continent whose very existence seemed at first to be the stuff of myth.

Opposite: **Gold was both the glory and the downfall of South American Indians as invaders lusted after objects like this cast gold flask in the shape of a seated woman. From Colombia, it is dated AD600–1100.**

Below: **The icons of the pre-Christian Indians reflected the world that surrounded them, including creatures like the puma, shown here as an incense burner, from Tiahuanaco, on the Bolivian border.**

The First South Americans

Nobody knows for sure when the first humans arrived in South America. Recent evidence suggests the presence of people as long ago as 30,000BC, though in terms of human history, this is recent. In Africa, Indonesia and China, for example, there is evidence of human settlement some 200,000 years ago.

Almost certainly the newcomers arrived from the north, for the original Americans were not indigenous to the continent. Instead they came from Asia sometime after 35,000BC, when an ice age lowered sea levels and created a land bridge over the Bering Straits between Russia and Alaska. The inhabitants of North and South America were thus originally related, as the many parallels between their respective mythologies would suggest.

At first the ice must have hindered the newcomers' progress southwards. But when a passage did eventually open up, they found a hunters' paradise in the North American heartland. The vast herds of bison, musk ox and mastodon grazing the plains probably provided little incentive for settlers to move on deeper into the New World. Perhaps it was overhunting that eventually drove them south into Mexico, where archaeologists have dated bone fragments back to 21,000BC.

On present evidence, another 10,000 years were to elapse before South America was peopled extensively, though the fact that the earliest remains yet discovered were found in Patagonia in the deep south suggests that the process may already have been under way for some time. The first settlers found a continent inhabited by species that are now long gone, among them the armadillo-like glyptodon and the mylodon – a giant sloth more than five metres long whose remains have been found penned up at the back of caves for all the world like cattle ready for slaughter. There was even prototheres, an early horse. Like the other creatures, it was hunted to extinction, leaving the llama as the continent's biggest beast of burden until the Spaniards introduced the modern horse many millennia later.

Then as now, the western part of the South American continent was dominated down its length by the Andes mountains, one of the Earth's highest ranges with peaks soaring abruptly to almost 7000 metres. To the east, rainforest cloaked most of the land above the twentieth parallel. South of that line, the wooded hills of what is now southern Brazil gave way to the barren plains of the chaco, to the pampas grasslands and finally to the sparsely-populated plains of Patagonia and the subarctic islands of Tierra del Fuego.

All these regions were to be inhabited in time, though the societies that evolved in them developed in radically different ways. The rainforest, with its luxuriant, at times almost impenetrable tropical vegetation but poor soil, sheltered small groups who learned to become one with its complex ecology, hunting game and gathering tropical fruits. The lifestyle they grew accustomed to was to change little over 10,000 years, and their successors live in a similar way today.

The chaco and the pampas also became populated with warrior tribes that supported themselves by hunting and agriculture. Here too, the environment allowed its inhabitants to maintain a stable lifestyle for centuries.

The Andean Crucible

It was in the west that South America's most complex indigenous civilization developed, and its focus was in the central Andes. At first sight it seems an unlikely place for a culture to take root, for unlike the lush river valleys of ancient Egypt or Mesopotamia it has always been a land of both physical and climatic extremes. Along its length

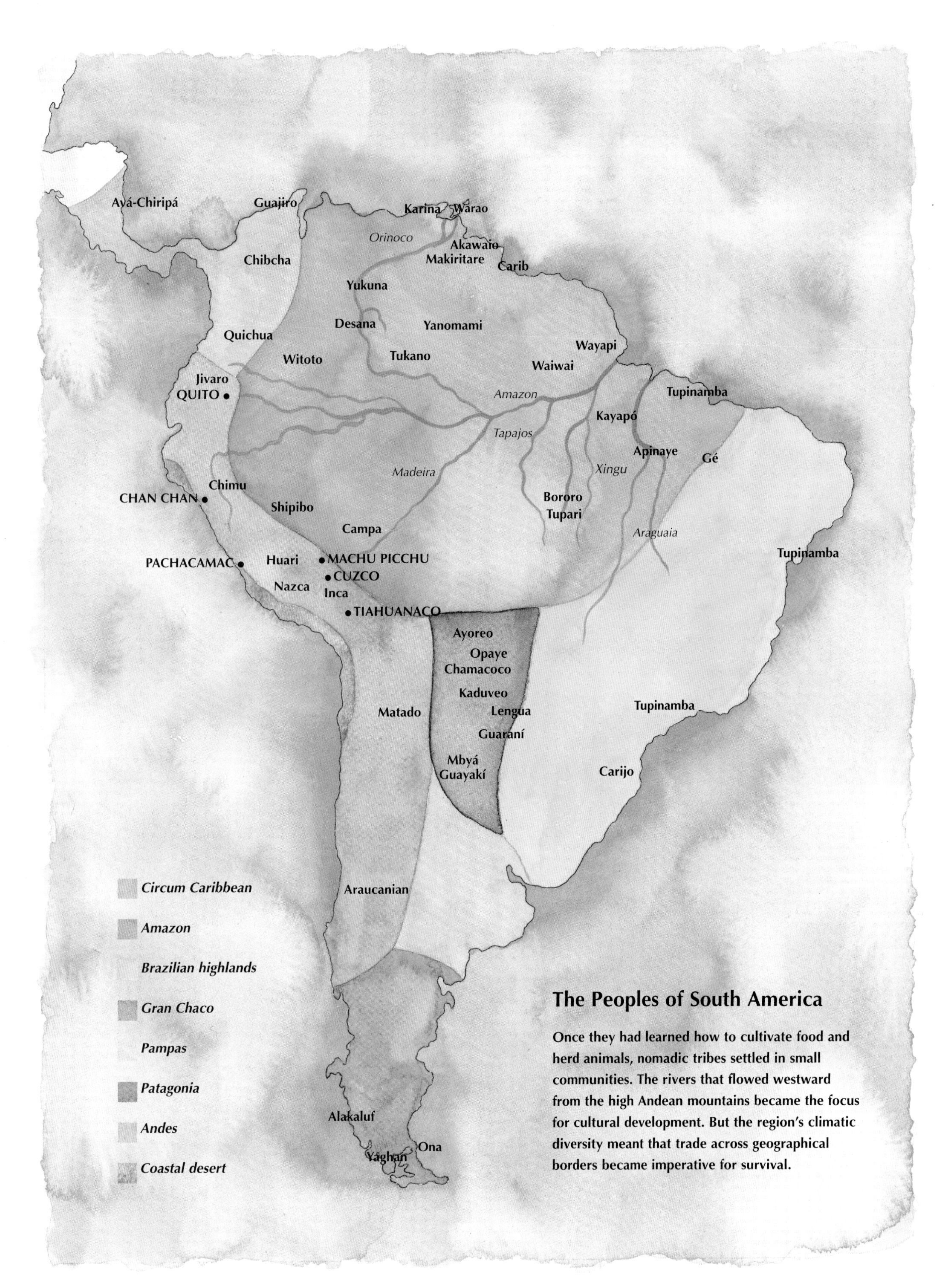

The Peoples of South America

Once they had learned how to cultivate food and herd animals, nomadic tribes settled in small communities. The rivers that flowed westward from the high Andean mountains became the focus for cultural development. But the region's climatic diversity meant that trade across geographical borders became imperative for survival.

the mountains reared up precipitously in a series of ridges running parallel with the coast. Between the peaks and the sea stretched a coastal plain that under normal circumstances could have been expected to be fertile, watered by rain borne in from the Pacific. But off the coast normal expectations are reversed by the presence of the Humboldt Current, a stream of cold water sweeping up from Antarctica that brings with it air temperatures colder than those onshore. As a result, winds do not carry rain inland; instead, they head out to sea, drawing moisture from the soil in the form of mist. The effect is to make the coast one of the driest regions on Earth. Parts of the Atacama Desert in northern Chile have a precipitation officially listed as zero.

Yet rain carried from the Atlantic side of the continent does fall plentifully on the Andean summits. To the east, the runoff is profuse enough to supply the Amazon, the world's biggest river. Even though less water falls away down the mountains' westward flanks towards the Pacific, there is still sufficient to supply a dozen or more major rivers whose flow is relatively constant throughout the year. These rivers, rarely much more than 150 kilometres long in their passage from mountain-top to sea, were to be crucial to the development of South American civilization. For it was on their banks that settlements developed and Peruvian civilization was created.

The peculiar geography of these valleys shaped the lives of the people who inhabited them and gave the cultures of early Peru many of their special qualities. They were separated from one another by wide stretches of barren desert, ecological boundaries that forced them to rely on trade with their neighbours for basic commodities.

Then there was the valleys' diversity. The steep fall of the rivers meant that they presented a whole range of climatic and agricultural conditions from high-peak to coastal all within a few dozen kilometres' distance. Over the centuries, this variety encouraged agricultural experimentation and led the peoples of the central Andes to become experts in irrigation and land management. Yet, all the valleys were ultimately dependent on the mountain hinterland for their water supply and so for their people's survival.

Although there is still disagreement about dates and locations, archaeologists have pieced together a general overview of the development of Andean civilization. In the third millennium BC, increasing numbers of hunter-gatherers began to settle. They often chose to make their homes at river mouths, where they lived in small dwellings made of stone or adobe brick, the roofs made of timber and whalebone. They went fishing on rafts made from inflated sealskins or lashed bundles of reeds, and supplemented their catches with the tubers and beans that grew wild in the region. In time they learned how to grow cotton and weave

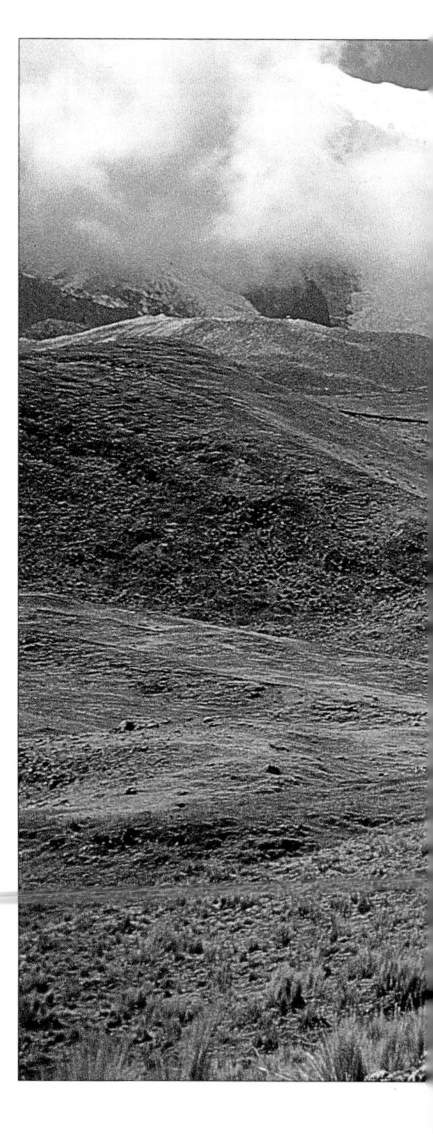

Until the Spanish introduced horses and cows in the 16th century, the llama was the only beast of burden on the continent capable of carrying loads weighing up to 45kg. Llamas thus became crucial to the expansion of trade routes, as well as providing sources of food and clothing. As such, they played an integral part in the growth of Indian culture, and sights such as this one, in the Bolivian Cordillera Real, have been part of the landscape since the dawn of Andean civilization.

garments from undecorated cloth, and to cook by dropping food into pots filled with water and warming it with heated stones.

At some unknown time, these people started building shrines – artificial mounds faced with stone in which they also buried their dead. A distinctive feature of these early holy places was a hearth or firepit. This contained a sacred flame to which offerings were made; analysis of the pits has turned up animal bones, seashells, lumps of quartz and the remains of chilli peppers.

An agricultural revolution began with the cultivation of quinoa – a plant with seeds like rice and leaves like spinach – and then, sometime in the second millennium BC, with the cultivation of maize which may have come south from Mexico. Soon maize became the staple crop, vastly improving the reliability and increasing the quantity of their food supply.

Well-stocked storerooms provided people with time for pursuits other than simple subsistence. Pottery first made its appearance in about 1800BC. Meanwhile the cultivation of maize and other crops on the arid coast inevitably created a new demand for the efficient management of water resources. Ambitious irrigation schemes were undertaken. At one settlement a huge canal, six kilometres long, was built, opening up many new areas for cultivation.

The co-operation required for such projects as well as for the management of communally-owned herds of llamas and vicunas – a wild

species of the llama genus – encouraged the development of *ayllus* – clusters of dwellings linked by strong ties of kinship. Great ceremonial buildings started to appear, often planned in a U-shape around open-ended courtyards facing the rising sun, suggesting a solar cult. By about 1400BC, the entire central coastal region of Peru was also linked by trade routes. The country was ready for its first great civilization.

Cult of the Jaguar Priests

Chavin culture is best described as a shared artistic style. It takes its name from a site 3000 metres up on the Andes' eastern slopes, near the present-day village of Chavin de Huantar. There the remains of a large, windowless building made of huge stone blocks still stand in front

The creature depicted in this embroidery, the so-called Oculate Being, was one of the region's earliest deities. This textile is from Paracas, Peru, and dates from *c.*600–200BC.

TIMELINE
South American History

Early South American society was marked by the rise and fall of cultures that provided an artistic or religious focus for the various disparate communities they influenced. Because the demise of most of these cultures remains a mystery, their exact dates are elusive. The groupings given here, therefore, are approximate but serve to illustrate the periods of ascendancy until the time of the Inca empire and the coming of historiography with the Spanish.

Valdivian fetish, 4000–1800BC

of a ceremonial plaza comprising two sunken courtyards, one within the other. Inside the main structure, which is ventilated by air-shafts, a maze of galleries and chambers link up via stairways. At the heart of the oldest section, two of these corridors intersect at a point that is marked by a five-metre-high statue of a sacrificial knife, now known as the Lanzon or dagger. Carved on this statue is a stylized image of a big cat – possibly a puma, more likely a jaguar. Its lips are drawn back to reveal its tusk-like fangs.

The Chavin temple was not the first building erected in the style that has come to bear its name, but it was the largest and most impressive, leading archaeologists to speculate that it was the focus of an extensive cult. If so, the movement seems to have originated in the north of Peru and spread southwards during the course of the first millennium BC. In the areas where it flourished, the U-shaped courts of earlier times were replaced by symmetrical plazas and walls decorated with huge stone reliefs. The sculptures generally represented deities that were linked to exotic and dangerous creatures of the rainforest – snakes, cayman, or eagles. And everywhere was evidence of the jaguar god, apparently the most significant deity of the new religion.

The Chavin style spread throughout the central Andes until by about 400BC it covered the entire northern half of the country. Then, for no known reason, it went into decline. It remained influential, though, and the fanged god was not forgotten. His image was passed on to successive cultures, along with another deity, the Staff-bearing God, so-called for the rods, each as tall as himself, that he held in his hands.

More than a millennium was to pass before the Andes region was again to have such a widely-diffused religion. In the meantime the culture of the Andes retreated into its constituent parts. Each region developed its own distinctive character with its own mythology, costume, rituals and customs.

The people of the Paracas peninsula on the south coast of Peru, for example, devoted much of their creative efforts to the celebration of death. These people were fine weavers and fierce warriors, and they buried their dead in shrouds decorated with the image of a god typically

35000–1BC

Nazca pottery mug showing figure with headdress and arrows

c.35,000 People migrate across the Bering Straits to North America.
c.30,000 Humans settle in South America.
c.2000 Nomadic tribes begin to settle, developing agriculture and textile and pottery making.
c.1400 The need for materials from other cultures leads to a network of trade routes throughout coastal Peru.
c.850–200 Chavin culture spreads throughout the entire northern part of Peru.
c.600–400 Growth of the Paracas empire on southern coast of Peru.
c.370–AD30 Growth of Nazca culture, which lasts for another 400 years.

AD1–1525

c.1–600 Moche culture flourishes, with pottery the foremost artistic expression.
c.500–900 The twin cultures of the Huari in the north and Tiahuanaco further south dominate the Andes.
900 Chimu nation rises on the north coast of Peru and remains highly influential until the advent of the Incas. At its height their capital, Chan Chan, covers some 20 square kilometres.
1230 Manco Capac becomes the first Inca ruler at Cuzco.
1438 Pachacuti becomes the Inca ruler and begins the expansion of his kingdom which until then stretched barely beyond the walls of their capital.
1471 Tupac Yupanqui continues his father's process of expansion.
1525 Civil war breaks out after Huayna Capac divides his kingdom.

AD1527–1881

1527 Francisco Pizarro arrives with his band of soldiers.
1532 Atahualpa is captured by the Spanish, precipitating the downfall of the Inca empire. The Inca leader orders the death of his rival Huascar, from his prison cell.
1553 Pedro Cieza de Leon publishes *La Cronica del Peru.*
1609 Publication of the *Royal Commentaries of Garcilaso de la Vega.*
1650 Population of Andean *altiplano* down to one million from the five million who lived there a century earlier.
1881 Araucanians finally subdued by Spanish.

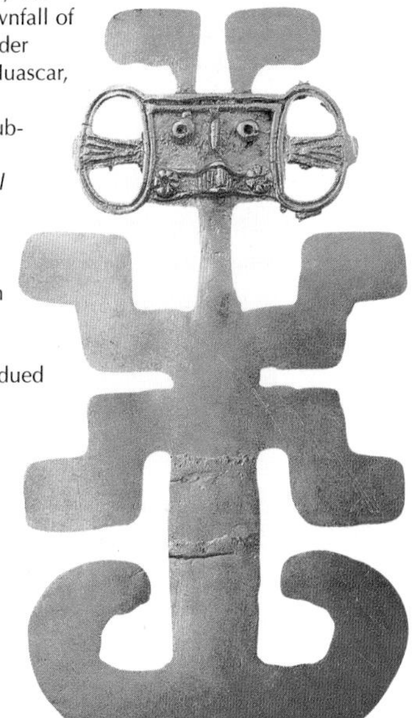

Anthropomorphic pendant, from the Tolima culture, Colombia, AD100–900

adorned with the heads of enemy tribesmen. His goggle eyes have led modern scholars to dub him the Oculate Being.

The people of the Moche valley in northern Peru left vivid records. They are remembered for the work of their potters, who modelled a miniature clay world that gives a vivid picture of daily life in the mid-first millennium AD when their culture flourished. Moche pots show lords on their thrones, mace-wielding warriors, fishermen in reed boats and healers treating victims. They also graphically depict some less appealing aspects of Andean life: roped captives awaiting sacrifice or, in one instance, a bird pecking out the eyes of a prisoner whose ears and nose have already been sliced off, possibly as a punishment for theft.

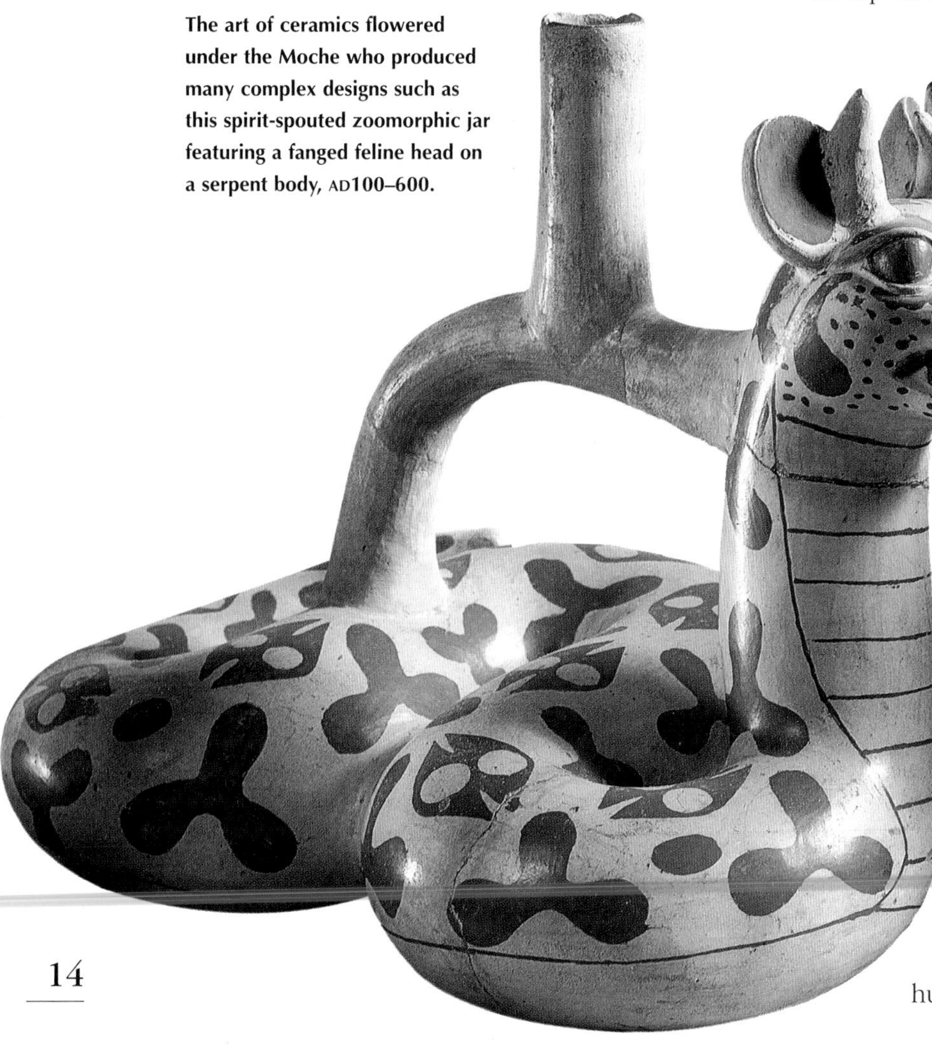

The art of ceramics flowered under the Moche who produced many complex designs such as this spirit-spouted zoomorphic jar featuring a fanged feline head on a serpent body, AD100–600.

The Moche could afford the luxury of art pottery because they had turned their valley into a model of agricultural productivity. Although meat was scarce – the only sources were duck and guinea-pigs, kept for eating – they grew maize, potatoes, beans, avocados, peppers, peanuts, manioc and squashes, and for fruit had guava, papaya and pineapple. Deer, which were hunted with the aid of dogs and beaters, seem to have been the sole preserve of the Moche aristocracy.

The Moche achieved their plentiful harvests partly by fertilizing their fields with guano, collected from offshore islands, and also with a complex system of irrigation works which increased the amount of land under cultivation. The culmination of this process came with the construction of a canal that cut across fifty kilometres of desert to tap the waters of a neighbouring river. These communal efforts turned the valley into what one Spanish chronicler described as "a veritable garden".

Political power went hand in hand with growing affluence, and Moche influence spread up and down the coast. They were fierce fighters, armed with maces, spears and copper-headed axes. Ceramics indicate the fate of their victims. Some were hurled over precipices, probably in sacrificial rites. Others were roped together and led to the great ceremonial plaza in the Moche valley where they would have their throats slit or their heads cut off.

Because of the absence of writing, little is known of the gods to whom these human offerings were made. They seem to have included not only the old Chavin fanged god but also a sun deity, who was often represented as an athletic huntsman in pursuit of game.

Children Born for Sacrifice

Many South American peoples offered sacrifices to their gods, and for some, human victims were the most valued offerings.

Archaeological evidence suggests that human sacrifice had a long history in South America. Moche pots from the 1st millennium AD show naked prisoners being killed on top of pyramids or on mountain summits in front of fanged deities. The Chimu made regular sacrifices, offering up children to propitiate the moon goddess.

The Incas regularly featured sacrifice in their ceremonies, though usually the victims were llamas or guinea-pigs rather than humans. At special times, however, they immolated children – 200 are said to have been put to death when a new emperor came to the throne. There were strict rules for the ritual. The victims, mostly adolescents aged between ten and fifteen, had to be physically perfect. They were feasted and made drunk so they would go to their death happily. Then they were led before a statue of the deity and strangled with a cord or else had their throats slit. Usually the ceremony took place in the temples, but the mountain connection was evidently not entirely lost. In recent decades climbers have stumbled upon caverns more than 5000 metres up in which richly-garbed boys as young as seven had been buried alive as sacrificial offerings to the sun.

A young man, seeming to accept his fate, is sacrificed to a feline deity on this Moche jar, AD1–700.

What is certain is that the Moche devoted great effort to worshipping them in fitting style. The ceremonial centre in their principal settlement was built on a giant scale. Its largest structure, bigger than any monument in Europe, was dubbed by the Spaniards the Pyramid of the Sun. It stood forty metres high and took more than fifty million adobe bricks to build. It contained rooms decorated with lively and playful frescoes, as did the slightly smaller Pyramid of the Moon which it faced; there, a fresco showed an army of animated clay pots on the march, brandishing weapons.

The Nazca Mystery

Another culture, almost 1000 kilometres to the south, left an altogether more enigmatic legacy. The Nazca people, who lived inland on a plateau traversed by the river of that name, chose to express their creativity in the unlikely medium of the surrounding desert. There they traced patterns, sometimes several kilometres long, by scraping away the rocks and dark surface gravel to reveal the lighter sand underneath.

In places they created dead-straight lines stretching for as far as twelve kilometres. With the stones that were cleared in their making piled up at the sides, these look from ground level very much like paths, perhaps leading to unmarked sacred sites in the wilderness. Elsewhere, however, they etched out abstract spirals and zigzags and vast sand-pictures – a dolphin, a gigantic hummingbird, a monkey with a swirling tail. The mystery of these elaborate, carefully-traced images is that although they can be viewed from the surrounding hills, their true magnificence is only evident from the air – a view that was well beyond their creators. There has been much speculation

A god-figure looks out from Tiahuanaco's Gateway of the Sun. The city, built in around AD600 at an altitude of more than 4000 metres, is one of South America's largest archaeological sites.

about the possible purpose of the Nazca lines since they were first spotted from an aeroplane in the 1920s. Their enigma has spawned many eccentric theories (see box page 35).

While the Moche and Nazca cultures were at their peak in the lowlands, a new centre was rising to prominence high up on the Andean spine. The obstacles in its path were formidable, for the *altiplano* – the high plateau cradled between the eastern and western *cordilleras*, or ranges – is one of the highest inhabited regions on Earth, with few villages below 3000 metres. To survive comfortably at such heights, the human body has to adapt. To this day the inhabitants of the region are barrel-chested, with extra-sized lungs and hearts twenty per cent larger than the norm. In addition their blood has more than the usual ratio of red corpuscles to aid the transfer of oxygen.

Tiahuanaco's Weeping God

Much of the *altiplano* is arid, but precipitation around the Peru-Bolivia border is enough to create the continent's largest inland body of water, Lake Titicaca, which is the remains of a much larger prehistoric sea. It was just twenty kilometres to its south that the great city of Tiahuanaco rose to prominence (see pages 44–45). In the absence of written records, historians have only been able to speculate about the lives of its people and the nature of the gods they worshipped. Archaeological evidence suggests that at its peak the city may have had as many as 40,000 inhabitants, subsisting on fish from the lake and on cold-resistant plants like the potato and millet-like quinoa, grown with the aid of irrigated, raised fields. Another crucial resource were the herds of llama and alpaca that grazed on the surrounding grasslands. The alpaca provided wool for the warm clothing needed at these heights, while the llama – the region's only beast of burden capable of carrying sizeable loads – enabled the Tiahuanacanos to maintain a monopoly of trade along the mountain spine. They consolidated their influence through military expansion and by creating a religious centre which continued to exert its influence well beyond its own demise.

Unlike the coastal dwellers, they had access to unlimited quantities of stone, which they shaped with a skill that still impresses modern engineers. Today traces of six architectural complexes survive, the largest of them 200 metres square at its base. Some of the stones used in its construction weighed as much as ninety tonnes, and were dragged by human effort from quarries more than five kilometres away.

Of all Tiahuanaco's former glories, the only structure to have survived the test of time relatively unscathed is the precinct's ceremonial entrance, dubbed by the Spaniards the Gateway of the Sun. Carved from a single, massive block of stone, it is dominated by an image of the Staff-bearing God – probably the same figure as was worshipped in Chavin times and almost certainly the city's patron deity. Beneath each of his eyes is a pair of small circles thought to represent tears. What the significance of the weeping god might have been is no longer known, but archaeological evidence suggests that his influence was felt for hundreds of kilometres up the Andean range and also along the Pacific coast.

One reason for Tiahuanaco's wide reach may have been the close links its people seem to have struck up with the Huari people, the other dominant force in Peru in the latter half of the first millennium. The Huari capital was a city of the same name located almost one thousand kilometres north of Tiahuanaco up the Andes spine. From this base they set out on a course of military conquest that brought the Moche and Nazca people under their sway along with many others, until finally they controlled much of Peru – a feat unparalleled up to that time. For unknown reasons, the Huari empire collapsed in the course of the ninth century, though their Tiahuanacano allies continued to prosper for another century or more after their fall.

For the next five hundred years, power in the central Andean lands once again split asunder. Control legally reverted to numerous independent statelets, few commanding much more than their own valley. Yet from their feuding ranks, one people who achieved a long-lasting fame were the Chimu, who ruled a short-lived confederation of cities scattered over the coastal plains of northern Peru and southern Ecuador. Their own capital, Chan Chan, was South America's largest city before Spanish times, a spectacular metropolis which at its height covered an area that stretched to twenty-four square kilometres.

Children of the Sun

By the mid-fifteenth century, the Chimu had been replaced by a much greater power. Yet the beginnings of the great Inca race could hardly have been more humble. According to their own legends, their first home was in the Lake Titicaca region, and throughout their history they looked back on the ruins of Tiahuanaco as the mysterious place of origin of their own culture.

The stories tell that they moved away from the lake under the leadership

The artistic craftsmanship of the early cultures is illustrated by this Huari-style fibre hat, from south Peru, decorated with stylized human faces.

of the first Inca – the name they also gave their ruler. Named Manco Capac, he followed an order from the gods to take his people northwards until they reached a spot where a golden rod that they carried with them was swallowed up by the ground. When they arrived at the site of Cuzco, their future capital, the rod sank out of sight in the fertile soil and the wanderers knew that at last they had found a home.

Even so, their very survival was a matter of doubt for years to come. Over the next two centuries, they maintained a precarious existence in a realm that never extended more than a few kilometres from their capital. The change in their fortunes came with the accession of Pachacuti, the ninth ruler in succession from Manco Capac. After repelling an assault by enemy troops on the capital itself, the warrior-prince forced his father to abdicate and embarked on a career of conquest. As the Incas themselves told the story, he did so under the influence of a vision in which the sun god Inti appeared to him and showed him, in a magic crystal, images of the lands that

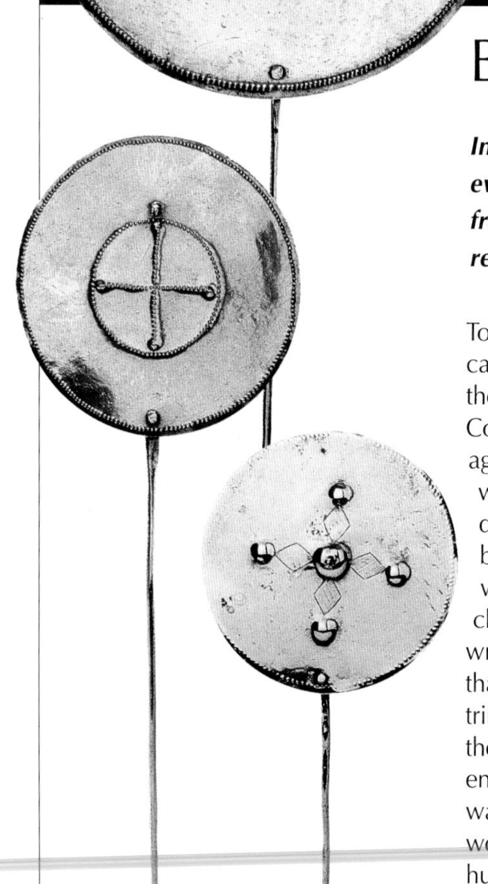

Beyond the Inca Frontiers

In the course of their expansion, the Incas conquered almost everyone with whom they came into contact. But on two frontiers they encountered peoples who, for very different reasons, they decided to leave well alone.

To the north, the Inca advance came to a halt beyond Quito in the rainforest of southern Colombia. There they came up against primitive tribesmen whom they regarded with distaste. "They were dirty, badly dressed and covered with vermin," the Inca chronicler Garcilaso de la Vega wrote of one group, reporting that the Incas had made the tribesmen pay a louse tax after they had been conquered to encourage them to mend their ways. Another group were even worse "since they feasted on human flesh". Finding little profit in making further progress in that direction, the ruler decided to call a halt to any further campaigning.

The situation in the south was very different. Fighting their way through Chile, the Inca armies found themselves up against the Araucanians, a fierce warrior people who fought them to a standstill in a battle that lasted three days at the Maule River. In later years the Araucanians were the only South American people who were able to resist the Spaniards successfully, managing to retain a degree of independence in their southern homeland until they were finally subdued in 1881.

The "chosen women", or *mamaconas,* were concubines of the Inca emperors, and were often buried with them. This gold figurine of a *mamacona* with a multicoloured cloak was found in a tomb, and reflects the esteem in which such women were held. She dates from *c.*AD1430–1532.

he would subdue and make the Incas' own. Pachacuti ruled for thirty-three years, until 1471, when Tupac Yupanqui, his favourite son, succeeded him. By the time of Tupac's death, twenty-two years later, the Inca realm stretched from southern Colombia to the Maule River, halfway down the length of Chile. And the empire, almost a million square kilometres in extent, had been stitched together by a complex network of common laws, roads and structures, and by a formidable bureaucracy which ensured the smooth running of the Inca state.

But for all its sophistication and its concern for the welfare of its subjects, Inca rule shared the weakness of all autocracies in that it was totally dependent on the will of one man. Under Tupac Yupanqui's son Huayna Capac, the fragility of the system became apparent. When the time came to nominate an heir, he proved unable to choose between two of his sons, one of whom was established in Cuzco, the other in the northern capital of Quito. So instead of deciding, he proposed dividing the empire between the pair. This solution pleased neither and on his death, a savage civil war broke out.

In the ensuing fighting, Atahualpa, the claimant from Quito, soon got the upper hand. To strengthen his position, he had many of his own relatives killed – Huayna Capac had been promiscuous, and there were reportedly three hundred of them to be dispatched – before advancing on Cuzco where his chief rival, Huascar, was entrenched. The stage was set for a bloody finale to a conflict that Atahualpa, who had the greatest support, was almost certain to win.

The Coming of the Conquistadors

And then something entirely unpredictable occurred that in a remarkably short time was to put an end to the whole Inca world. Word reached Atahualpa that a band of strangers had arrived on the Pacific coast. At first there seemed little cause for alarm. An envoy sent to size up the foreigners reported that they did not seem to be great warriors and that a force of merely two hundred troops could overpower them. The Inca, who could call on many thousands of tried and tested soldiers, saw no reason for fear.

What he did not know was the determination of the newcomers or the fact that they brought with them weapons against which he and his fighters had little defence. Francisco Pizarro and his band of 168 fortune-hunters were Spanish conquistadors, and they were set on emulating the feat of their compatriot Hernan Cortés, who had brought down the mighty Aztec empire in Mexico just eleven years earlier. They dreamed of winning fabulous wealth, and were prepared to stop at nothing to achieve it.

The denouement was swift in coming. Atahualpa invited the Spaniards to his camp at Cajamarca, where he and his army were resting en route to Cuzco. There, on November 16 1532, he went with an escort of more than 5000 unarmed men to visit the strangers. Pizarro and his men were waiting with guns and loaded cannon. In the ensuing massacre, Atahualpa was captured.

As a ransom, the ruler agreed to fill a forty-five-square-metre room more than head-high with gold and silver. Although he carried out the promise, it was not enough to save him. The treasures only showed the Spaniards how much gold there was in the country. After garroting their royal captive, they set out to make themselves

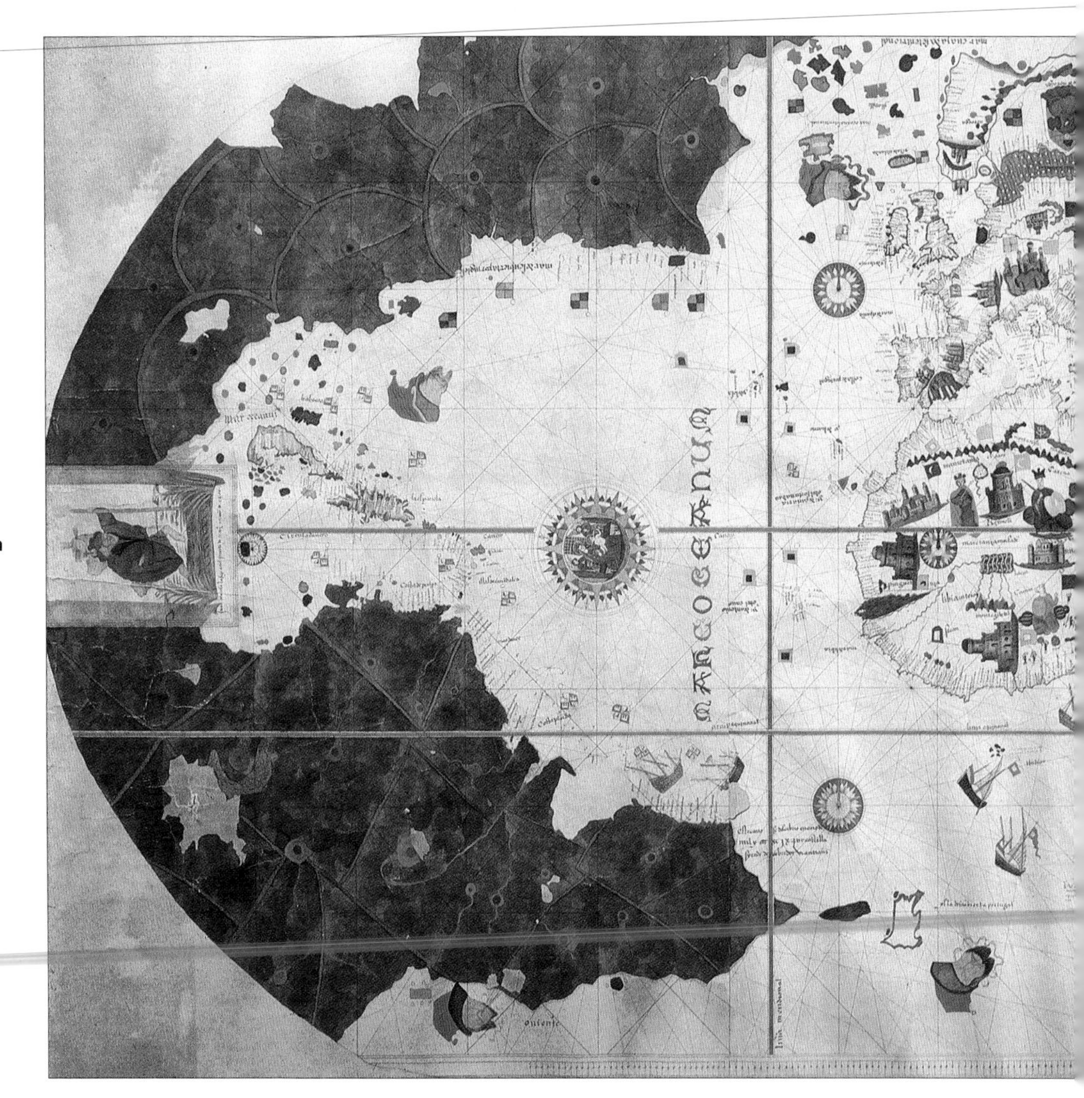

Stories of the impossible riches offered by South America ensured Pizarro was not the last of the European adventurers to explore the region. Even while Peru was being conquered, the Portuguese were establishing themselves in Brazil, and other conquistadors tried their luck in Colombia and Venezuela to the north. From Peru, exploration south into Bolivia and Chile was simple so that by the 1550s Europeans were established in all but the very south of the continent. This map, by Juan de la Cosa who was with Columbus in 1492, shows the New World in AD1500.

Plundering the Temples of the Gods

The conquistadors who seized control of the Inca empire had one over-riding passion: the lust for gold. And one of the easiest ways to satisfy it was to plunder the temples of the Inca gods.

When Pizarro and his men captured the Inca Atahualpa, the ruler made an attempt to buy his freedom by offering to fill a room in the fortress at Cajamarca with gold as high as a man could reach. According to the conquistadors' own accounts, it was Atahualpa himself who suggested the temples of Cuzco and Pachacamac as the best places to find the precious metals.

Pizarro's half-brother, Hernando, led the raid on Pachacamac, a pre-Inca shrine long famed for its oracle, situated on the coast of Peru. He was disappointed by the treasures he found there, and it seems likely that the priests, hearing word of his coming, had removed and hidden them before his arrival. The Spaniards had more luck in Cuzco, where 700 golden plates lined the walls of the temple. And when the panels were melted down, each contained, on average, two kilograms of pure gold.

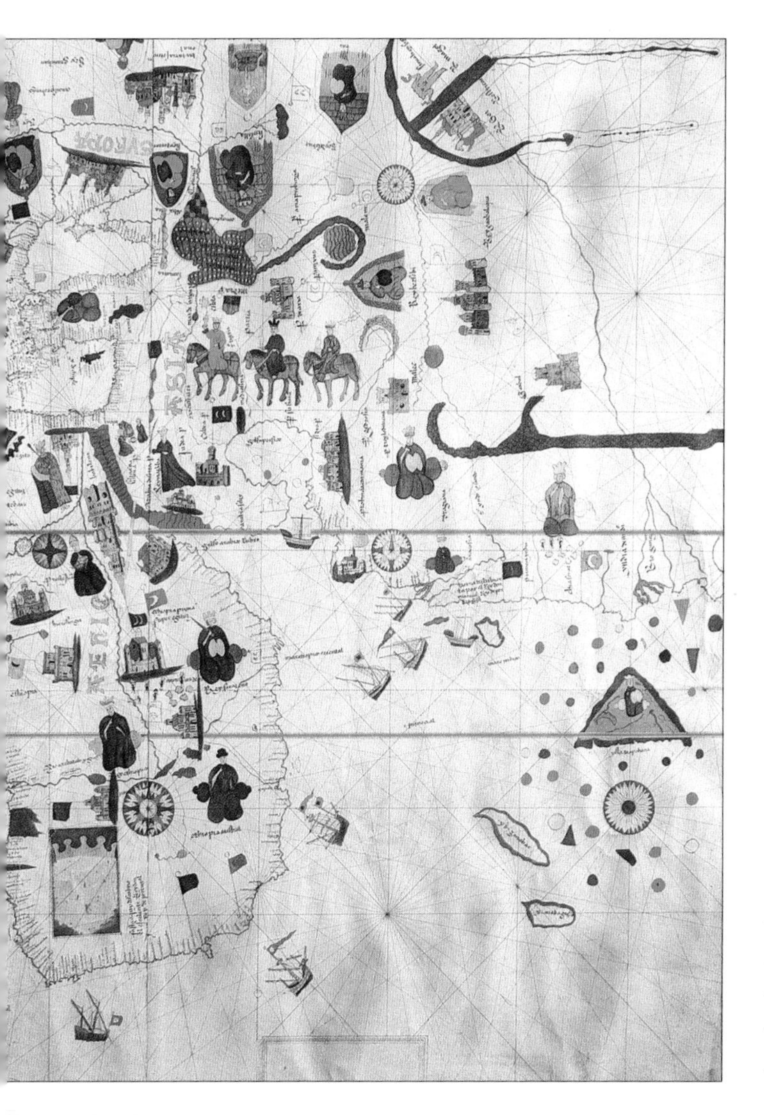

masters of the entire empire. And they succeeded at a speed well beyond their wildest dreams.

With Inca opposition in such disarray, victory was not difficult to achieve. So deep were the divisions carved by the civil war that Atahualpa, even when imprisoned by the Spanish, had arranged for Huascar, his rival, to be assassinated, rather than trying to organize any joint military effort against the common enemy. And what resistance the Incas could muster was further weakened by the ravages of European disease that took many more lives than the guns and steel-tipped lances of the invaders. Within a year of the massacre at Cajamarca the invaders had taken the Inca capital of Cuzco. Thereafter, though they fought among themselves and continued to face native resistance for another forty years, the Spanish grip on the central Andes never weakened.

Pizarro's triumph in Peru was soon followed by other conquests. Even before his victory the Portuguese had established a permanent settlement on the coast of Brazil. While Pizarro was advancing on Cajamarca, Colombia and Venezuela were being conquered. In Venezuela, the Spanish colony of New Grenada was to be created in 1538. Buenos Aires had been founded two years earlier by an expedition from Spain, opening the way for the future colonization of Argentina. Peru itself provided a springboard for the conquest of Bolivia, and Chile followed in the 1540s. By mid-century Europeans were established throughout the continent except for the far south, where they ran up against the resistance of the Araucanians (see box page 18). Even though much of the interior remained beyond their reach, there was no longer any serious challenge to their supremacy. In effect, the whole of South America had been turned into an Iberian colony.

The effects of colonization were mostly disastrous for the native people. Their societies were dislocated, their ruling classes swept away and for the most part their customs and beliefs were suppressed. Traditional religious practices were proscribed and missionaries fanned out through the newly-conquered lands to spread the message of Christianity in their place. Demoralized and bewildered, the Indians also fell victim in huge numbers to unfamiliar European diseases to which they had no immunity. In the Andean *altiplano* alone, it has been estimated that the native population declined in the century from 1550 to 1650 from five million to under one million.

A Living World of Belief

Yet despite the great and calamitous changes, the native culture of South America was not entirely crushed. One of the most important developments was the introduction of writing by the Spaniards. Much of what is now known of early Andean mythology was in fact preserved by the first chroniclers. While some were native to the Andes, many of them were European churchmen seeking to understand the mindset of their new converts. One result is that the myths of many peoples have come down to us through an

Guardians of the Past

News of Pizarro's exploits and of Inca gold fired the European imagination. But few of the many books the new land inspired showed much understanding of its native inhabitants.

The Inca Achachi Apocamac shoots a jaguar in the jungle. This 1565 drawing is by Guaman Poma de Ayala who provided the only pictorial account of life in the Andes in the 16th century.

The first Spanish accounts from Peru justified the actions of the conquerors. But within ten years of Atahualpa's capture, a soldier-chronicler named Pedro Cieza de Leon began travelling through parts of Colombia, Ecuador and Peru taking notes on what he saw. His work, *La Cronica del Peru*, appeared in 1553 and featured a bitter denunciation of the murder of Atahualpa by his captors.

Other key authors include Guaman Poma de Ayala and Garcilaso de la Vega whose *Royal Commentaries*, published in 1609, offered the first truly Inca perspective. The son of a Spanish conquistador and an Inca princess, Garcilaso lived from the age of twenty-one in Spain, but he identified strongly with his mother's people, and called himself "El Inca". Although historians now criticize his book for its lack of objectivity, it was, in its day, a singularly powerful cry for a culture that had been all but demolished and a people who had long been oppressed.

Inca prism, for the Incas happened to be the dominant power throughout the region when the age of literacy dawned. While scholars can only speculate about the exact significance of the Chavin jaguar god or the Paracas Oculate Being, they can consult early Spanish sources to find out what the Incas themselves said about their creator god Viracocha or the great sun god Inti.

For the old beliefs were never entirely forgotten. Even in regions where the European presence was at its strongest, these beliefs lingered on underground, often making their presence felt under a superficial veneer of Christianity. Elsewhere native beliefs survived intact in a bewildering variety of forms. For the fragmentation of the Indian population, particularly in the vastness of the rainforest, led to the development of numerous different variations on a common mythology. This allowed many gods, and tales about them, to flourish despite the new religious orthodoxy.

Even so, some patterns emerge from this confusion of divinities. Among them are striking parallels with the mythology of other parts of the world, particularly in the more northerly parts of America. Tales of divine brothers, close in spirit to the Hero Twins of the Maya of southern Mexico and Guatemala, crop up repeatedly. So, more mysteriously, do legends of a robed and bearded man from the East bringing with him the arts of civilization – a direct parallel with the Aztec stories of Quetzalcoatl. Accounts of a flood that destroyed almost all the human race can be found all over South America just as they appear in the mythologies of almost every other known region of the world. Most pervasive of all, particularly in the rainforest, is the belief in shamanism.

Living in a dangerous world, the Indians see themselves as under siege from the malevolent attention of hostile spirits. The influence of these invisible but lethal agents can only be counteracted by the skills of individuals who have special powers over the spirit world, the key to which is often found through the use of hallucinogenic plants. Some shamans are thought to be able to transform themselves into beasts, especially the feared were-jaguar. Others are renowned for their medical skills and healing abilities, and their services are called on whenever a member of the tribe falls ill.

So, in the timeless and mysterious world beneath the forest canopy, the beliefs still live on that first flourished in Siberia, the original home of shamanism, many thousands of years ago when the Bering land-bridge still straddled the Old and New Worlds.

This feather headdress, or *roiro ri*, comes from the Txuhahamae tribe, a sub-group of the Gé-speaking Kayapo, who live around the Xingu River in the Mato Grosso area of the Amazon. It would have been worn by adult men for various rituals, such as name-giving ceremonies.

LOST CULTURES OF THE ANDES

Among the high valleys and deserts of the Andes lie fragments of once great civilizations laid low by the slow march of history. One such culture is that of the Moche, a people who flourished within the austere landscape of Peru's northern coast from 400BC to AD600. While the mountains created a formidable barrier to both rainfall and trade, so they increased the need for tradable goods and irrigation. The myriad sculptures and ceramics which have survived the Moche testify to their success in meeting these challenges. They articulate a world both brutal and culturally refined as the people became as adept at irrigating soil as at fortifying vulnerable towns. Having secured a means of survival in the arid shadow of the Andes, the Moche were able to develop an accomplished artistic sensibility.

Left: **Part fox, part feline, this mythological creature was frequently depicted by the Moche. It dates from AD50–100 and is made from ceramic and mother of pearl.**

Above: **Catastrophic climate change in the 7th century AD devastated the Moche, burying their land beneath dunes. Yet the sand that destroyed the civilization preserved its finest artefacts.**

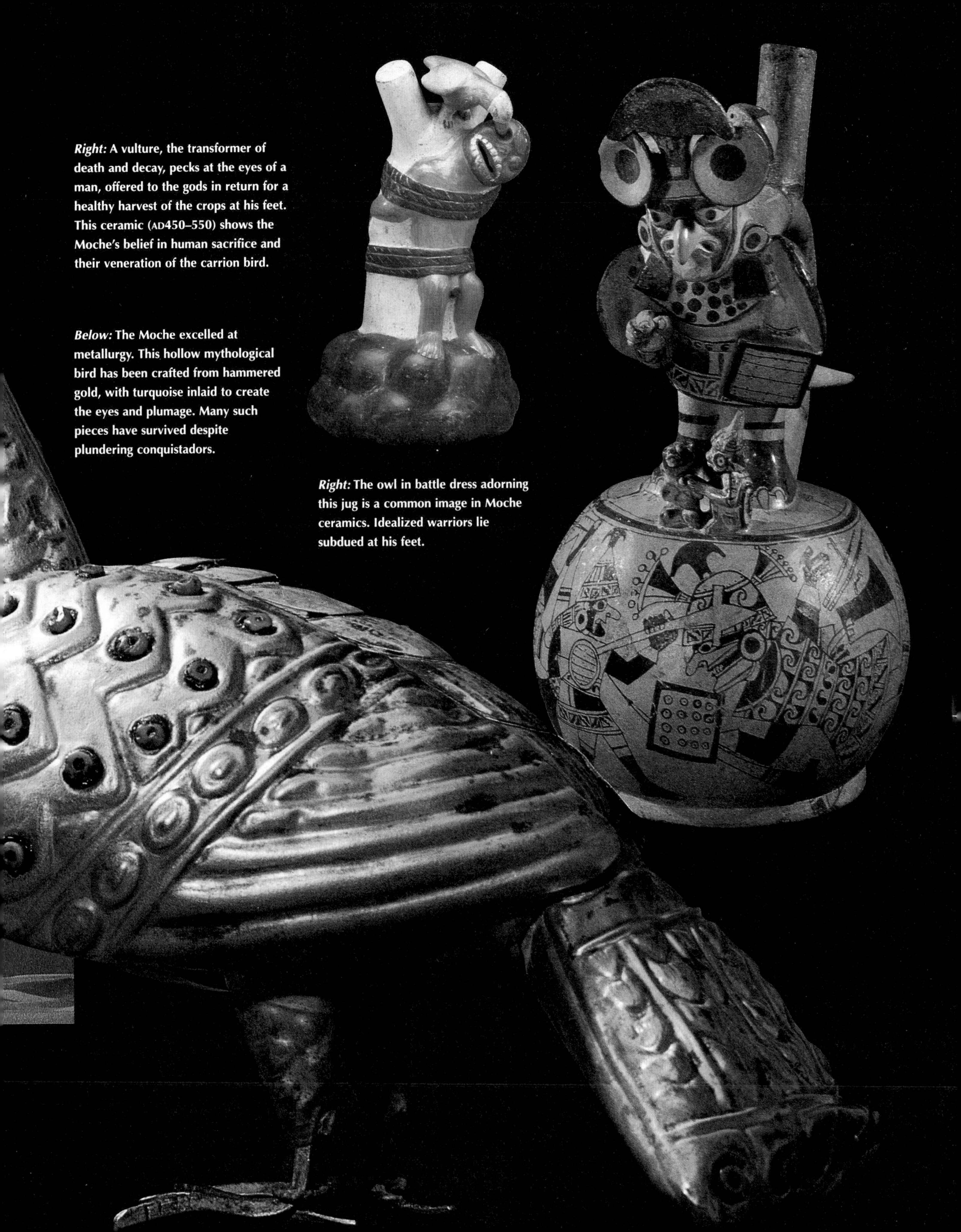

Right: A vulture, the transformer of death and decay, pecks at the eyes of a man, offered to the gods in return for a healthy harvest of the crops at his feet. This ceramic (AD450–550) shows the Moche's belief in human sacrifice and their veneration of the carrion bird.

Below: The Moche excelled at metallurgy. This hollow mythological bird has been crafted from hammered gold, with turquoise inlaid to create the eyes and plumage. Many such pieces have survived despite plundering conquistadors.

Right: The owl in battle dress adorning this jug is a common image in Moche ceramics. Idealized warriors lie subdued at his feet.

REALM OF THE CONDOR

The towering Andes mountain range runs for almost 6500 kilometres down the western side of the South American continent. From Colombia in the north to Tierra del Fuego in the south, imposing mountains overlook a dramatic range of landscapes. The grasslands, the dry coastal plains and fertile valleys, even the high, barren plateau of Callao in southern Peru, have seen several great civilizations rise and fall.

Before the Incas rose to power, the Chimu ran the state of Chimor in Peru, ruling for more than 500 years from Chan Chan, a place which, at its height, covered some twenty square kilometres. Then there was the majestic city of Tiahuanaco, set high on the austere *altiplano* ("high plateau") near Lake Titicaca. Here flourished a culture that spread its influence for more than a thousand years until it fell into decline after the first millennium AD.

But evidence of the Indians' patterns of belief is frustratingly sparse. Their myths were passed down by word of mouth and no written record was made until Spanish priests began recording local legends in the sixteenth century. Inca gods and myths have many antecedents among the earlier Andean cultures. Wherever the Inca empire spread, the conquerors adapted and subsumed local mythologies. Discovering the roots of these myths, therefore, is not easy, but by studying archaeological evidence it is possible to unravel some of the beliefs of the earlier cultures from Inca mythology. For instance the Inca god Pachacamac (see page 38) appears to have been a Chimu deity, and Viracocha seems to be closely allied to the creator Con Ticci (or Thunupa) worshipped by the Indians of the *altiplano*. Even the Incas' origin myth – that the first Inca emerged from islands in Lake Titicaca – was based on tales told by the Indians of the Callao plateau.

Andean mythology is thus rooted in the landscape. For tribe after tribe, the mountains, source of life-giving waters, are objects of awe and reverence. The Huarochirí Indians were not alone when they looked up to a snow-capped mountain peak and declared it Pariacaca – their chief god.

Above: **In the shaman's trance, shown in this Chimu textile, AD1000–1470, cacti have taken human form. Shamans throughout the Andes allowed tribes to mediate between the real and the spirit world.**

Opposite: **Landscape and culture were intimately connected for Andean tribes. Mountains featured strongly in the rich mythology of the region.**

Valleys of the Chibcha

The Chibcha, inhabitants of mountain valleys in modern Colombia to the north of the Inca empire, created a great civilization that survived until the Spanish invaders arrived in the sixteenth century. Three tribes – the Zipa, the Zaque and the Iraca – ruled the Chibcha lands. They believed that the universe was created by an all-powerful god named Chiminigagua.

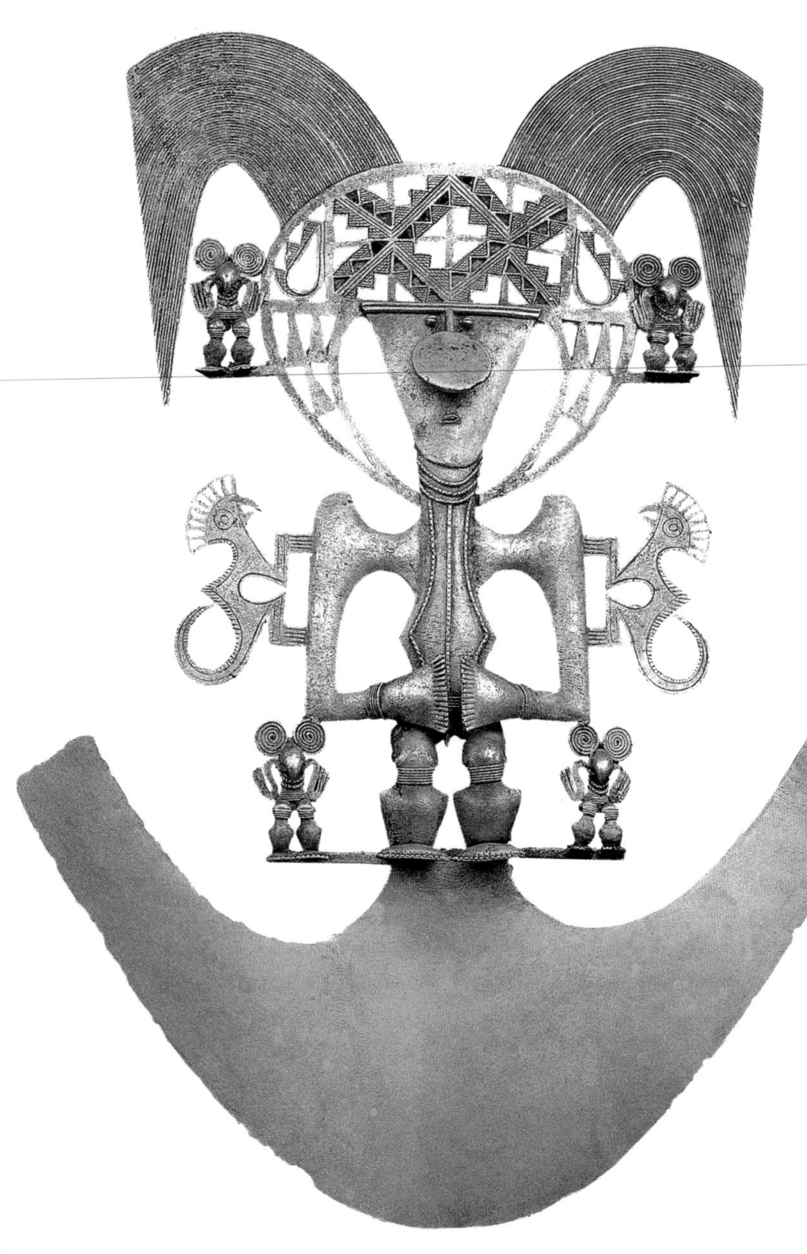

With a pectoral such as this adorning his chest, a member of the Popayán tribe, neighbours of the Chibcha, would have displayed his wealth and power. This piece dates from AD1100–1500.

In the first days, the Chibcha told, the Earth was covered in darkness. Then the god Chiminigagua, who contained shining light within him, began creation by setting the light free. First he fashioned a flock of great black birds that carried his light inside them and instructed them to fly through the world. As they soared over the towering Andes, they released the brilliance, like falling moisture, from their beaks and the world filled up with light. It was only afterwards that Chiminigagua made the Sun and set it in the sky, and created the Moon to be its consort.

In some versions of the myth, the light that Chiminigagua released was originally hidden inside a vast house over which he had control. After some time, he decided there had been enough darkness and set the light free. Chiminigagua, the Chibcha said, was also filled with goodness – and the first Spanish chroniclers of the native myths identified him with God the Father in the Christian tradition. But although Chiminigagua created the universe, he did not make mankind.

The First Men and Women

A little while after light had settled on the Earth, a woman named Bachue ("large breasted") clambered from Lake Iguaque high in the Andes, carrying her young son in her arms. He was three years old and just emerging from infancy into childhood. With him, she settled nearby and lived quietly, watching proudly as he grew into a handsome young man. In time she became his lover and proved so fertile – each of her pregnancies resulted in between four and six children –

Lakes were often seen as magical sites. The awe inspired by the "El Dorado" lake in Guatavita, Colombia, moved Chibcha chiefs to dive into its waters covered in gold.

that eventually the ever-multiplying family of her children and their descendants grew large enough to populate the entire Earth.

Bachue and her son lived together with their people for many years, but one day they felt an urge to return to the sacred mountain lake from which they came. Bachue called some of her people together at the lakeside and bade them farewell. She handed down laws governing day-to-day life and told them to live together peacefully and to honour the divine order. Then before their eyes she and her son transformed themselves into serpents and slithered away into the lake.

Ever afterwards the pair were worshipped – and were said sometimes to appear to their followers in a vision, as glistening snakes. Local people also threw offerings into the lake. Bachue – sometimes known as Furachogue ("kind woman") – became an Earth divinity, the Chibcha goddess of agriculture, harvest and water.

The belief that the first people came from a watery place – a sacred lake or stream – was common to many American peoples. In the Inca legends, for example, the first men came from Lake Titicaca in Peru (see page 65). The myth of Bachue is also linked to another common body of legends in which people came from beneath the Earth. The Chibcha Indians, indeed, believed that at the point of death, people's souls returned to the centre of the Earth, carried along the course of an underground river on featherweight canoes made of spiders' webs. For this reason, spiders were held in the highest regard.

Boredom Breeds Creativity

The Chibcha also passed down a variant history of how the first men and women were made. According to this tale, two *caciques* – native princes – were alive in the time of darkness at the start of the world. The *cacique* of Sogamozo and his nephew, the *cacique* of Ramiriqui, were surrounded by a great fog of darkness and grew bored. To entertain themselves, they took some clay and a handful of reeds, moulding the first men from the clay and cutting the first women from the reeds. They told their creatures to worship them faithfully and then, to provide light,

The rectangular style of this red ceramic Chibcha mask is distinctively Peruvian. The beasts which decorate its edge reflect the animal world from which, as Andean mythology saw it, the human race had come.

climbed into the sky, the prince of Sogamozo becoming the Sun and his nephew the Moon.

An ancient rite thought to be connected to sun worship may have grown from this myth. The ceremony took place at Sogamozo, the Sun's territory according to the legend. Twelve men dressed in red, perhaps representing the twelve months, danced around a man robed in blue, who may have stood for the sky or the sun. The dancers chanted a song recalling how people must die and be turned to dust but their souls would live on.

Chiminigagua created the universe, but he was not worshipped as the chief of the Chibcha gods. That honour fell to the sun deity Bochica, who was revered for giving the people civilization and knowledge of the arts.

According to legend, Bochica appeared from the east. He came in the form of an old man in full-length robes with long hair and a beard growing down to his waist. At this time the people were living almost as animals, without gods, buildings or even crops. Bochica taught them how to build huts and grow fruits, how to spin and weave and how to live together peaceably and sociably. He also instructed them in the worship of the sun god and persuaded them to lead chaste and sober lives. People flocked to hear him speak. At Cota he lived for some time in a cave and preached regularly to vast crowds of people.

But much of Bochica's work was undone by his beautiful wife Chia, sometimes known as Huitaca. A tall, comely woman, she followed him into the Chibcha lands, preaching the opposite of his doctrine. Where he encouraged the people to be chaste and sober, she told them to drink and dance, be merry and make love. It was a message the people liked to hear and many came round to her ways, but Bochica, naturally enough, was furious and prepared to stop her.

In some versions of the myth she provoked him even further by using her magical powers to make the Funzha River overflow its banks. It created a flash flood, which only a few people were able to escape by clambering on to the mountaintops. For his revenge Bochica banished her from daylight, condemning her to live only by night from that day to the end of time. Some histories relate that he turned her into the Moon; others that he made her into an owl, which shuns the sun and must fly abroad by moonlight. As Huitaca she became the Chibcha goddess of drunkenness and self-indulgence.

Bochica remained on Earth for 2000 years, living a life of self-denial and instructing the people in the ways of civilization. He established festivals, pilgrimages and sacrifices, and appointed a high priest for the cult of the sun. He also saved the people from a great flood (see box page 33) and from the terrifying god of storms, Thomagata – who, like Huallallo Caruincho, a god of the Indians of the Huarochirí region of Peru, took the form of a fireball. When at length he departed, he either ascended to Heaven or he left for the west, leaving his footprint in a rock.

Bochica was worshipped as the giver of laws, with precious sacrifices of gold, tobacco – and also boys. The victim, named the *quesa* ("wanderer"), was always taken from a particular village, now known as San Juan de los Llanos, that was connected to Bochica's cult. At the age of ten he was moved to a sun temple at Sagamozo and for five years he was treated with the greatest care and reverence. When he reached fifteen he was taken

Seeds of Life

One set of creation myths told by northern Andean tribes featured an all-powerful divinity named Sibu, who had the power to grow men and animals from seeds.

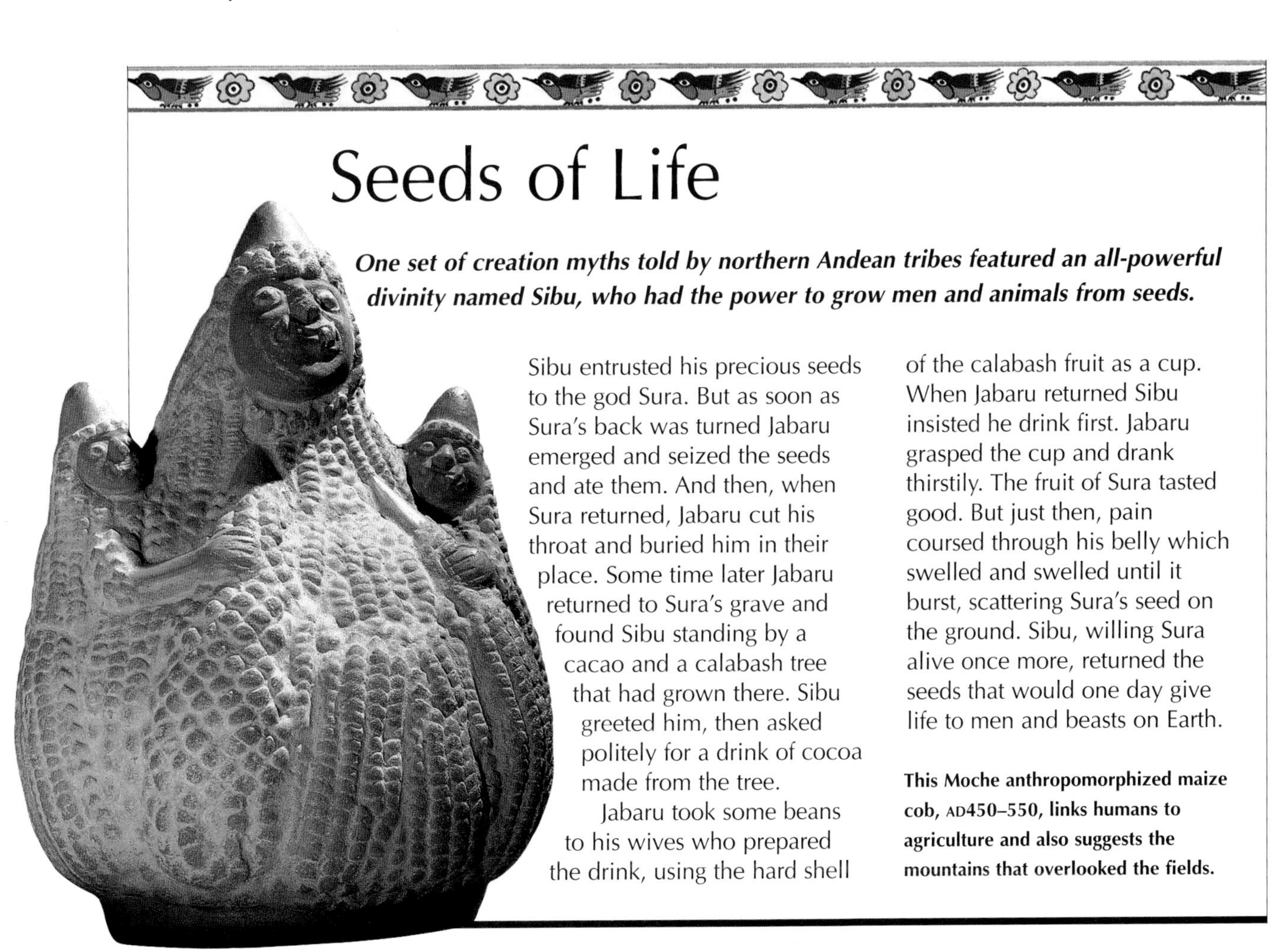

Sibu entrusted his precious seeds to the god Sura. But as soon as Sura's back was turned Jabaru emerged and seized the seeds and ate them. And then, when Sura returned, Jabaru cut his throat and buried him in their place. Some time later Jabaru returned to Sura's grave and found Sibu standing by a cacao and a calabash tree that had grown there. Sibu greeted him, then asked politely for a drink of cocoa made from the tree.

Jabaru took some beans to his wives who prepared the drink, using the hard shell of the calabash fruit as a cup. When Jabaru returned Sibu insisted he drink first. Jabaru grasped the cup and drank thirstily. The fruit of Sura tasted good. But just then, pain coursed through his belly which swelled and swelled until it burst, scattering Sura's seed on the ground. Sibu, willing Sura alive once more, returned the seeds that would one day give life to men and beasts on Earth.

This Moche anthropomorphized maize cob, AD450–550, links humans to agriculture and also suggests the mountains that overlooked the fields.

in a splendid procession to a pillar erected in Bochica's honour and shot dead with arrows by priests. After he had died, the *quesa*'s heart was cut out and offered to Bochica and the child's blood was collected as a sacrifice to the god.

Bochica was also known as Xue ("Lord"), Sugunsúa ("disappearing one") and sometimes even as Chimizagagua ("messenger of Chiminigagua"). The Spanish priest Pedro Simon, who in the seventeenth century recorded some of the myths and traditions of the Chibcha and other South American peoples, claimed that the cult of Bochica had grown from a folk memory of a visit by one of Christ's apostles.

Bochica is a type of the divine figure common in South American myths. Called a "culture hero" by scholars, he teaches culture and social and survival skills to tribes that were previously primitive. He is comparable to Kenos in the myths of the Tierra del Fuego tribes (see page 48) or the Chimu deity Pachacamac (see page 37). Different peoples gave the culture hero more or less divine status.

A Disgraced King

Bochica's sojourn in the Chibcha lands was used by local mythmakers to support the notion of divine kingship and to validate the ruling dynasties' hold on power. In the same way, legends of the first Incas were used further south along the Andean range in Peru (see pages 64–67).

The histories recount that at Sugamixi in the eastern part of the territories the ruler of the Iraca lands, Nompanem, warmly welcomed Bochica, and that the god established the laws and religious rituals in Nompanem's realm. Shortly afterwards the high priest Idacanzas founded a dynasty of priests for the sun cult – presumably with the visiting god's approval.

But Hunsahua, chief of Tunja, broke the divinely ordained conventions and suffered a terrible fate. He was overcome with desire for his own sister and found that she was all too willing to share the illicit pleasure. Flushed with happiness, the young lovers expected understanding from their mother – but she flew into a rage, declaring that she would never allow them to be together.

Hunsahua and his sister eloped. But when, after another argument with their mother, they left for the far south of their lands, horror followed them. At Susa, moments after Hunsahua's sister had given birth to a healthy baby, the child was turned by divine magic into stone. They travelled on to Tequendema, where Bochica had created a vast waterfall – renowned as one of the wonders of the world – when he dissipated the flood created by the god Chibchachum (see box opposite). Here they thought they might find solace for their pain and resolved to make their home, but they too were turned to stone where they stood in the middle of the fast-flowing river.

Divine retribution and death attended another Chibcha couple whose sexual appetites and pride brought them public shame. A chief at Lake Guatavita – where a temple stood to the serpent god who lived in the waters – discovered that one of his wives had been unfaithful to him with another man. In his rage, he ordered her lover's murder and then forced her to eat the dead man's sexual organs. He even paid musicians to sing songs about her faithlessness around the town.

The lady fled from the palace with her baby daughter and flung herself and the child into the lake. Now the chief regretted what he had done and he went to see his most powerful shaman and asked him to find a way of bringing her and the baby back to live with him. The shaman sacrificed to the god of the lake, then, after hurling heated stones into the waters, himself leapt into the deep.

The shaman discovered the lady and her baby alive and well on the lake bed, living with the serpent god of the waters, and he hurried back to tell the chief the wonderful news. When he heard this, the chief ordered him to go back and bring his wife and child home. For many hours the chief waited anxiously, but when the shaman finally returned it was only with the baby's tiny corpse. He told the chief that the serpent god in the lake's depths had eaten the child's eyes and so the baby had died.

The Anger of Chibchachum

The people of the Bogotá plain provoked Chibchachum, god of labourers and business, to a fury with their complaints and disobedience. In his rage, Chibchachum sent a great flood to wipe out the region, but the people appealed to the sun god, Bochica, to protect them.

Bochica appeared astride a rainbow that arched majestically over the local town of Soacha. He brought out the sun to dry up the waters, then took his gold staff and hurled it at Mount Teguendama, creating a chasm in the rocks through which most of the flood flowed away. The magnificent waterfall that Bochica made still exists today, spilling into the sacred Lake Guatavita.

Bochica was determined to punish Chibchachum and dispatched him to the Underworld with the task of supporting the world on his shoulders for eternity. Some accounts tell how it had previously been held up by pillars; others that it was kept aloft by trees. From time to time, the weight becomes too much for Chibchachum and he shifts it from one shoulder to the other – causing the Earth to shudder and grind in an earthquake.

The rainbow had marked the Chibcha people's deliverance from the flood, and ever afterwards they worshipped it as the goddess Chuchaviva. They prayed to be saved from the curse of Chibchachum who from his Underworld exile decreed that the rainbow's every appearance would also bring death. Bochica's wife Chia, who had tried to undermine his civilizing influence (see main text), may have lent her magic to Chibchachum to create the great deluge, for in other myths she is responsible for floods.

Creation and Deluge

All cultures have myths explaining how the world was created, but in addition the tribes of the Andes share tales of a great flood. Similar in essentials to the story of Noah in the Bible, the South American flood myths tell how one, two or sometimes a group of people escaped the deluge by climbing to the top of a mountain.

According to the Cañari Indians of Andean Ecuador, mankind was saved from total extinction by the intervention of a magic mountain. A great flood swept across the land and two brothers hurriedly gathered food supplies and fled the lowlands, taking refuge on Huacaynan peak. As they looked down fearfully at the mounting waters from their lofty perch, at first they could not understand why, although the flood was rising and other peaks were being submerged one by one, it appeared to be getting no nearer to them. Then the truth came to them; as the waters climbed, so Huacaynan grew taller to keep them safe. The brothers stayed on the mountain, surviving on their meagre supplies until the waters went down.

At first they were afraid to leave their place of safety, but they had eaten all their food and they had to go in search of more. They set off across the mountainside and walked until they dropped with exhaustion. They built a makeshift hut on the spot where they had collapsed and scratched a living gathering edible plants and roots. But every day was a struggle, for they never had enough to eat and were always hungry.

One evening, when they trailed home after a long day searching for food, they found a meal laid out in their hut together with beakers of *chicha* – corn beer. It looked like a feast prepared for a king and they ate and drank hungrily, once again unable to believe their good fortune. That night, for once, they slept deeply and well, without noticing the damp and cold of the mountain.

When they returned the following evening they found another feast, and again on the next day. The same thing happened for ten nights, and the brothers grew more and more curious as to the identity of their benefactors. After the tenth night, the two young men decided that they would set a trap. The elder brother volunteered to keep watch to see who came to prepare the food.

On the following day, when the younger brother left as usual to look for supplies, the elder one concealed himself in the building and settled down to wait. He fell into a reverie but he was disturbed by the flap of wings and, looking up, saw

While the spectacular landscapes of the South American interior tend to dominate Andean mythology, cultures whose influence stretched to coastal regions, such as the Chimu, also looked to the ocean for inspiration. In this piece of Chimu pottery, a crew takes to the sea guided by a totemic figurehead.

The Mysteries of Nazca

Giant images of animals, birds and people can be found etched in the ground at several places in Peru. The most famous are those created on a plateau in the Pampa de Ingenio Desert by the Nazca, who thrived from around 200BC to AD600.

In the pebble and sand of the desert's thick white soil the Nazca etched their mysterious patchwork of zigzags and spirals. Some form recognizable patterns – a plant, a whale, a giant bird, a monkey – while elsewhere lie long straight lines which can run unbroken for up to eight kilometres.

The lines were first discovered in the mid-1920s, but their meaning has remained hidden despite exhaustive research. German archaeologist Maria Reiche, encouraged by the American Paul Kosok, studied the lines for decades. Her theory, that the images were aligned with constellations and offered some kind of astrological guide to the seasons, remained popular until, in the late 1960s, the British astronomer Gerald Hawkins tested the theory with computers and found that actually very few patterns corresponded with the stars.

Various theories have been devised to explain why the images can only be seen from the air. The most eccentric of these was put forward by the Swiss writer Erich von Daniken, who in the 1970s declared that the lines were giant landing strips used by alien spaceships – whose occupants, he claimed, set up a base at Tiahuanaco some time around 600BC (see page 44).

Some writers have suggested that the lines may have been connected to religious rites and used by shamans – priest-doctors whose spirits were believed to have the power of flight. Others claim the Nazca had developed a primitive glider or hot-air balloon which they used to look down on their designs from the air. But most modern studies have argued that the lines were made not for viewing from the air at all but for walking or running on, perhaps during religious rituals. People may have gathered to use them in ceremonies designed to draw life-giving water from the sacred mountains above.

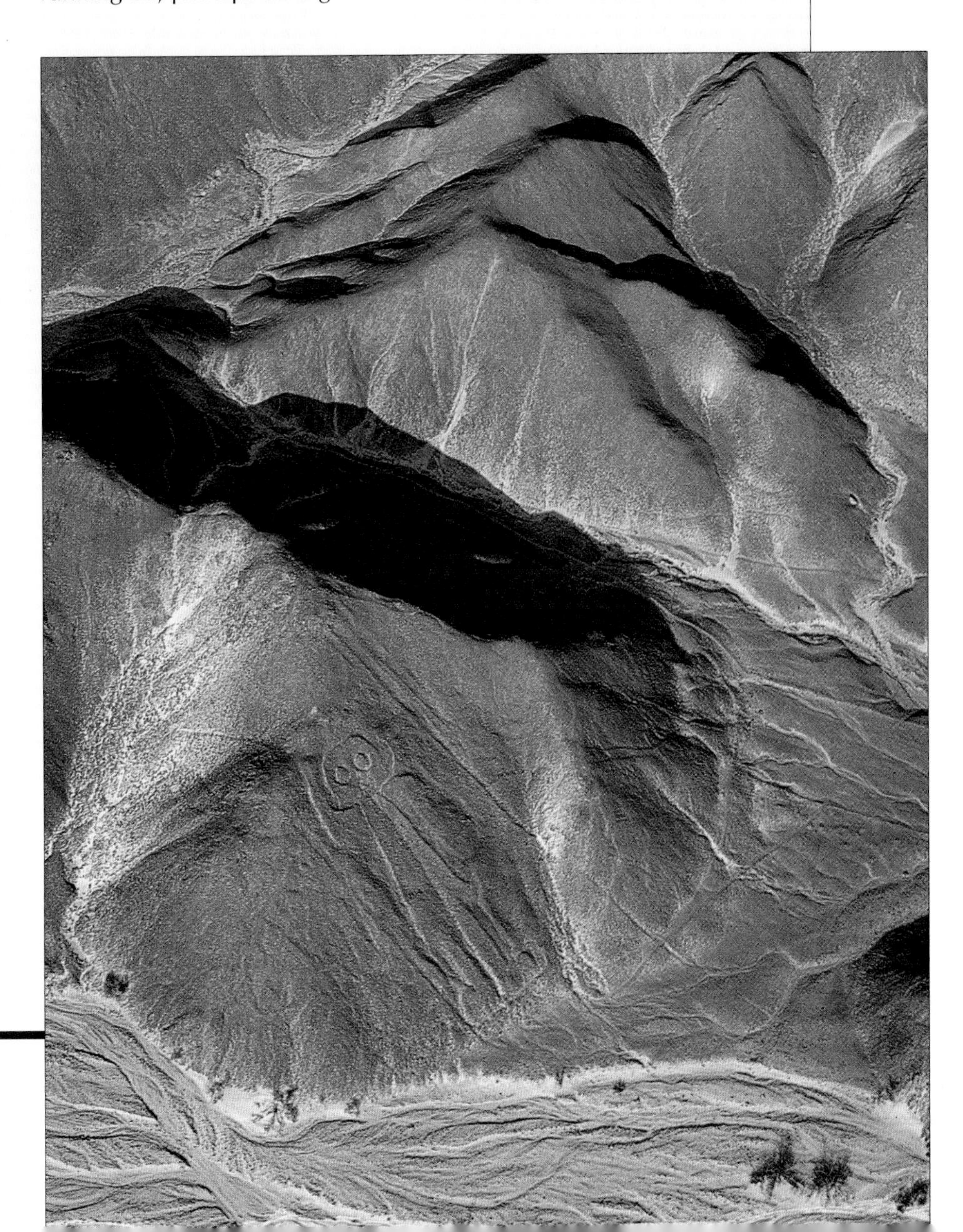

Human figures, like this one etched into a hillside in the San José pampa, are rare among the Nazca figures. However, they are thought to predate the drawings of animals and birds.

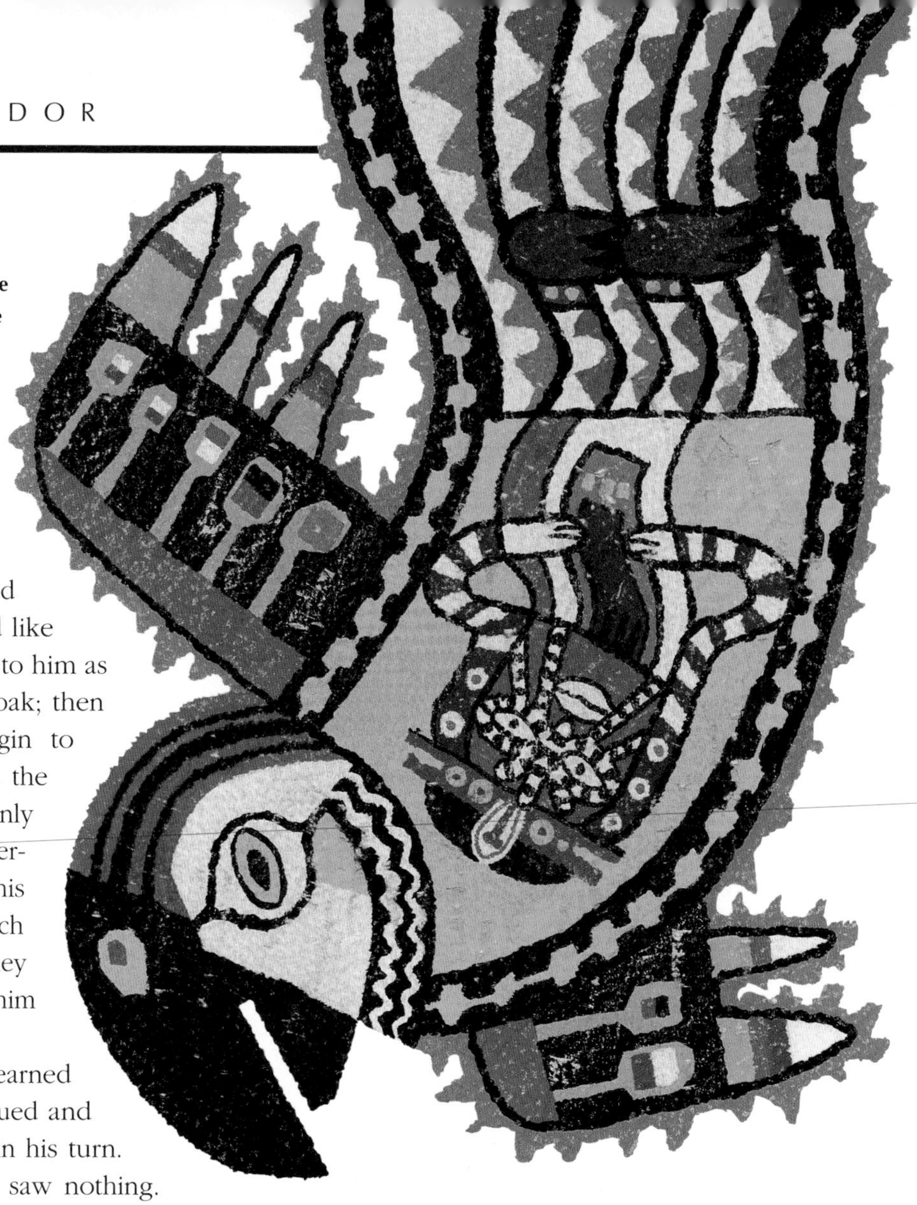

Disguised as a macaw, one of two beautiful bird-women flies down from her home in the heavens. She and her sister secretly tended the first men of the Cañari tribe – the only people to survive the great flood. The men fell in love with their tenderness and beauty.

two brightly coloured macaws come to land before the hut. He quickly understood that magic was at work because the longer he gazed at them, the more the birds looked like women of his own tribe. It seemed to him as if the larger bird was wearing a cloak; then he saw her take it off and begin to prepare the food. Both birds had the faces of beautiful women. Suddenly he could bear it no longer and, overcome with longing, he burst from his hiding place in an attempt to catch them. But with an angry cry they flew away into the sky, leaving him alone and hungry.

When the younger brother learned what had happened, he was intrigued and insisted that he would lie in wait in his turn. For three days he kept watch but saw nothing. On the fourth his patience was finally rewarded, for he heard the beating of birds' wings and saw the macaws circle the hut and then come down to land. It was just as his brother had said – they looked exactly like beautiful Cañari women.

He watched as they went inside the hut and made the food. As soon as they had finished, he rushed into the hut, shutting the door to trap them. Both birds screeched in fury. He managed to grab hold of the smaller while the larger one burst past him, knocked the door open and flew away. Intoxicated by his captive's beauty, the man made love to her many times. She had grown calmer when she saw that he intended to treat her well. Soon she became pregnant and in time gave birth to six sons and six daughters.

Afterwards the brothers lived with the bird-woman on the mountainside for many years. They were able to grow crops from seeds that she brought back in her beak from far away. The twelve boys and girls were the ancestors of the entire Cañari race. Ever afterwards the Cañaris regarded Huacaynan as a *huaca* – a holy place – and they had a special regard for the macaw.

The Chimu Flood Tale

The Chimu Indians who lived on the coastal plain of Peru and northern Chile also told of a great flood that wiped out most of mankind. This flood story may be based on a real El Niño event – a weather phenomemon which periodically brings catastrophic floods to the South American coast.

In the Chimu myth, the only survivors were a handful of men and women who clambered high into the mountains and hid with their animals and supplies in cold, damp caves beneath the peaks. After some time, their food ran low and they sent out dogs to see if the waters had subsided. On the first few occasions, the animals returned clean so they knew that the land was still flooded; but one day the dogs came back spattered with mud and then the people knew that the flood had receded.

They crept cautiously down the slime-covered mountain and built a new settlement, determined to get on with their lives. But, cruelly, many of the survivors were killed by a plague of poisonous snakes that thrived in the mud and filth left behind by the departing waters. A few hardy folk escaped, killed the snakes and set to work repopulating the world.

The plain occupied by the Chimu is largely barren, but is punctuated by fertile valleys where precious water flows down from the mountains. Here the Chimu created the majestic city of Chan Chan, heart of the great Chimor civilization that finally fell to the Incas in the fifteenth century. The Chimu had to learn to make the most of their water supplies and developed complex irrigation systems. One of their creation myths explains how the land came to be as it is.

Con and Pachacamac

In the first days of the world, before men had been created, a god named Con came into the land from the north. Strong and lithe, he could move quickly over the most difficult terrain. Wherever an obstacle blocked his way, he simply removed it by the power of his will, decreeing that mountains should sink or valleys be filled as he desired. His father was the all-powerful sun.

But Con was lonely, so he created men and women and set them down in a pleasant, fertile land. At this time grain was easily harvested and fruits ripened quickly, and the first people had an easy life, wanting for nothing. But some of them angered Con and, swelling with divine indignation, he resolved to make their lives difficult.

He ordered the soft rains to stop so that the plush grasslands were transformed into a stony

Prominent noses and large eyes animate these ritual Chimu drinking vessels. Crafted from single sheets of silver, the cups, dating from between AD1359 and AD1476, were buried with a nobleman. It was believed that they would bring him sustenance after death.

The Wonder of Pachacamac

At the mouth of the Lurin River stood a temple whose cult proved so enduring that when the Incas stamped their authority across the Andean landscape, imposing their own code upon its disparate cultures, they decided to allow the cult of Pachacamac to remain, and drew it into their own great cult of the sun.

There were few unifying features in South America in early times. People lived in small communities, their identities shaped by their immediate environment. What cultural focus there was, however, came not from a political structure, but from the rituals at the great temples: Chavín de Huántar, Tiahuanaco and Pachacamac.

The influence of Pachacamac in particular spread far beyond its own Lurin valley. It was the only temple dedicated exclusively to the creator god of the same name and pilgrims would come with gifts from miles around to pay their respects or consult the shrine's revered oracle.

After crossing the inhospitable mountains, travellers would be awed by the temple, lying as it did on a man-made hill set within its fertile coastal valley. Fantastic murals covered the adobe walls and through its many doors access could be found to a series of plazas. The shrine itself was the preserve of nobles, priests and pilgrims who would have to fast for twenty days to gain admittance to the lower plaza; for a whole year for entry to the upper. Above this inner sanctuary rose a terraced pyramid at the top of which was found the oracle itself, the wooden idol around which the cult of Pachacamac turned.

People would come to consult the oracle on all important issues, from the prospects of the year's harvest to matters of personal health and welfare. Failure to follow its advice would lead to all manner of natural disasters. But only priests could enter its chamber, consulting it on others' behalf, and even they were prevented from casting their eyes upon the idol by a cloth that hung before it. And the god was appeased by the blood of regular sacrifice.

From the lands that lay beyond the Lurin estuary would also come petitions for a local shrine to Pachacamac. And, if successful, the local community would be sent a priest. In return they would offer up a stretch of land, its produce used for offerings to the cult. Each new temple was seen as a child of the cult whose family, which knew no boundaries of culture or degree, survived the might of Inca domination.

The riches collected in the temple were buried to keep them from the plundering Spanish, and included this llama-wool cloth decorated with a bat motif. It pre-dates the Incas' rise to power.

desert and at a stroke turned their rich, generous land into a barren one where nothing would grow easily and quickly. But looking at his people labouring hopelessly over the hard, stony ground, Con felt a moment's pity and decided that if they were willing to work hard he would give them a little help. He decreed that at some places rivers would flow down into the plain from the mountains behind, bearing precious waters from the melting snow. The people learned quickly to dig irrigation canals and were able to scratch a meagre living from the soil.

But Con's reign was disturbed when a second god came into the land. This newcomer, called Pachacamac ("Creator"), was the child of the Sun's union with the Moon, and so one of Con's brothers. Pachacamac immediately began to challenge his brother's authority. After a tremendous struggle, he prevailed and drove Con out. Then Pachacamac wandered throughout the land he had won, deciding what he wanted to do with it.

Much of what he saw pleased him. But Pachacamac decided he was not impressed with the people that Con had made, so he transformed them into a breed of chattering monkeys and sent them off into the wilds. He then created a new people, and these were to become the worthy ancestors of the men and women who are alive today. He taught them all that they know – about hunting and farming and about the arts and the family. In return the people made Pachacamac their supreme god and worshipped him faithfully, building a great temple in his honour near the Peruvian city of Lima (see box opposite).

When the Incas conquered the coastal kingdoms they imposed their laws and their culture, but they also took over some of the gods of the people they defeated. Pachacamac and his brother Viracocha were among these gods, and they both became important deities in the Inca pantheon. In some accounts Pachacamac is described as a tall, white man with the power to do magic and even work miracles, who proclaimed that people should show each other love. Spanish churchmen used to suggest that this myth – like that of Bochica (see page 30) – may have had its roots in a visit to South America by a Christian apostle long before. They liked to suggest that Saint Thomas made his way to the continent from Palestine by way of eastern Asia. This theory, though, is far-fetched, and smacks of the kind of revisionism the Christian fathers were keen on.

The nurturing of souls beyond the grave was an important feature of Andean life, as shown by this wooden figure found at a Chimu burial site. Several layers of plaster have been applied to its face, a sign of spiritual regeneration. In its hand is a *kero*, a ceremonial drinking vessel, further suggesting that the figure, dating from around AD1000, was used in rituals.

In the Shadow of the Gods

The Huarochirí region covers part of the western flank of the Peruvian Andes, and the myths handed down by the local Indians were connected intimately to the landscape. Like other groups they viewed the mountains as sacred places; the name of their chief god, Pariacaca, is also that of a snow-capped peak that was revered as his home.

For many years anarchy ruled over the Earth. But while tribes battled for survival, with no great leaders or kings, five eggs quietly appeared on the highest slopes of Condor Coto mountain. They contained the great god Pariacaca.

In the lands beneath the peaks lived Huataya Curi. Although a poor peasant, only he knew about Pariacaca's appearance – for he was the god's son. One day, Huataya Curi was returning from the ocean when he grew tired and lay down to rest. In his sleep he heard two foxes talking about a rich man named Tamtanamka who had been taken ill and whom no one had been able to cure. According to one of the foxes, his wife had been unfaithful to him and this was why the man had fallen ill. She had been toasting maize when a grain had leapt out of the fire and burned her dress in the most intimate place. She had then given the grain to the man she desired and they had made love. That grain had spawned a hideous double-headed toad that lay hidden beneath Tamtanamka's grinding stone. And ever since their union two snakes had hung from the eaves of his house devouring all of Tamtanamka's strength.

Huataya Curi resolved to go and find the invalid and cure him. At the man's house he met a beautiful young woman who sadly told him she

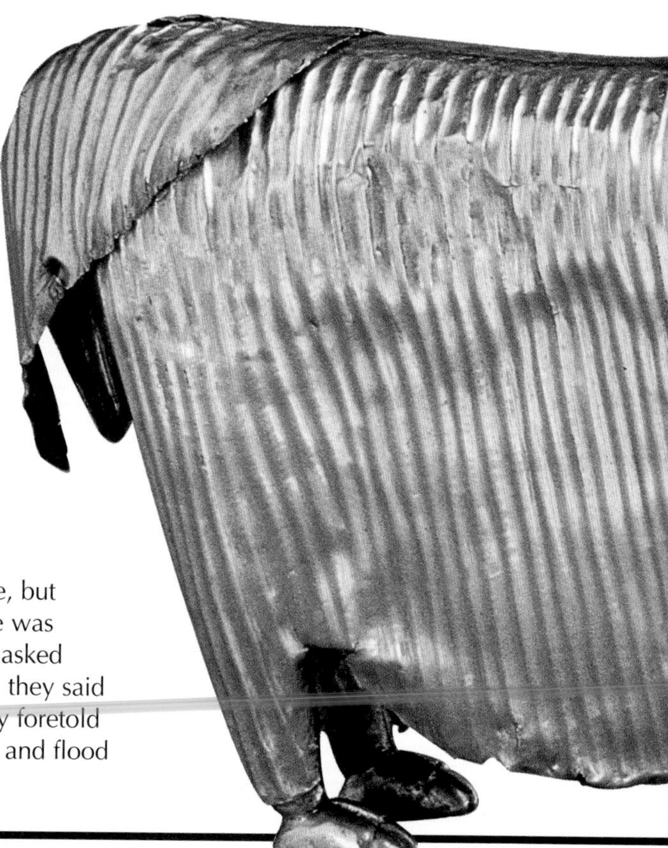

The Llama

The llama was a great friend to the Andean Indians. It was a hardy pack animal, its wool kept men and women warm and its flesh fed them. They even made candles from its fat and shoes from its skin.

The Indians believed that the souls of the dead were sometimes reincarnated as llamas and they often sacrificed the animals to the gods. Llama wool, fat and even foetuses were used in sacrifices. Some Indians even believed that llamas had the power to see the future – as in one version of the deluge myth that was told on the Peruvian coast.

A shepherd took his llamas to a rich pasture, but they would not eat. He was troubled and when he asked them what was wrong, they said that a portent in the sky foretold that the sea would rise and flood the Earth for five days.

was the sick man's daughter. He told her his purpose and she took the stranger to her father.

Huataya Curi told Tamtanamka that he would cure him if he could marry his daughter. And the desperate lord agreed. Huataya Curi then told Tamtanamka of his wife's adultery and the creatures in his house. Kill these beasts, he said, and the sickness will depart; on recovery, worship Pariacaca, who would be born on the next day.

When Tamtanamka's servants found the snakes in the roof, his wife confessed. Then Huataya Curi found the toad under the grinding stone. Tamtanamka's illness left him and he at once allowed Huataya Curi to marry his daughter.

The Huarochirí saw the llama cast in the Milky Way, not as a constellation but in the dark spaces between the stars. This is just one of the many examples of their reverence of the animal, shown here represented in crimped silver sheet.

The Trials of Huataya Curi

But Huataya Curi's problems were not over. His new brother-in-law was indignant at the match. Vowing to humiliate the peasant who had married his sister, he challenged him to a contest. At this time Pariacaca appeared on Condor Coto and Huataya Curi travelled to meet his father. He told Pariacaca of the brother-in-law's challenge and Pariacaca said that he would help him. The

The shepherd asked his flock if there was any way of escaping the flood, and the llamas told him to gather enough food for five days and then to drive them to the top of the great Villacota mountain. He did as he was told and when they arrived at the peak they found that it was already crowded with animals, but no people. Too busy with their own concerns they had failed to spot the portents.

No sooner had the shepherd and his flock reached the summit than the waters began to rise. The fox could not keep his tail from getting wet, and it was stained black for ever. But after five days the waters subsided, as the llamas had predicted. The animals and the shepherd returned home, and from that lone survivor all the people in the world are descended.

In some versions of the myth the shepherd took his six sons and daughters with him to the mountain top, and the peak – as in the tale of the brothers told by the Cañaris (see main text) – rose higher and higher to escape the rising waters. This certainly makes it easier to explain the repopulation of the Earth after the deluge.

brother-in-law first suggested a music and drinking contest. Pariacaca told Huataya Curi where to find a fox's panpipes, a skunk's drum and a small-necked jar filled with *chicha,* corn beer, on the mountainside. With these implements Huataya Curi made such powerful music and provided so much drink that he was declared the winner.

When the angry brother-in-law next proposed a dressing-up competition, Pariacaca gave his son a fine suit of snow and he won again. And the same happened with a third trial – the wearing of exotic lions' skins. With Pariacaca's help, Huataya Curi soon appeared dancing in a magical red skin beneath a rainbow. The villagers gasped and applauded, and Huataya Curi was once again declared the winner.

In desperation, the wealthy man next suggested they race to build a house. He had many workers to help him, but Huataya Curi, for all his magic powers, only had his wife. The wealthy man's helpers almost completed the entire building on the first day while Huataya Curi had done no more than lay the foundations. But when the sun rose the next morning, there stood Huataya Curi beside a veritable mansion. In the night the animals, birds and snakes had helped him build it.

Now Huataya Curi declared that it was his turn to choose an activity. He challenged his rival and his wife to a dancing contest but they had barely begun to show their steps before he turned them into deer and set off in pursuit. He caught the wife and stood her on her head so that her skirt fell down, exposing her private parts. Then he turned her to stone and, ever since, passers-by have stopped to stare at her. And although the wealthy man escaped into the mountains, he was cursed to live out his life as a deer.

Pariacaca, God of Waters

Pariacaca emerged from the eggs on Mount Condor Coto in the form of five falcons. After flying far and wide, the birds returned to earth and took human form. Some say the five people are Pariacaca and his four brothers, but others that they are different forms of the god.

Pariacaca was a deity of mountains, water and wind, and several stories describe him launching great floods. In one he destroyed a village with a deluge because when he passed through at festival time nobody offered him a drink. He also used water to seduce the beautiful maiden Chuqui Suso, whose maize was dying from lack of water. Pariacaca told her he would make water flow freely into her fields if she would make love to him. Later they walked together beside a canal named Coco Challa where she turned into stone. In May during the canal cleaning season even today Indians hold a festival of drinking and dancing in Chuqui Suso's honour.

The toad was one of the most poisonous beasts of the Andes, with a prominent place in the Indians' supernatural menagerie. This piece, from AD100–200, gives the toad jaguar markings.

Distant Shores of Paradise

The Huarochirí told tales of a time when their home was a fertile paradise – before the god Pariacaca drove them out into drier lands. Scholars believe that the Indians may once have lived in lush valleys nearer the coast but were defeated by invaders and driven inland to the harsher highlands.

The Indians in those days were ruled by two holy people or gods named Yana Namca and Tuta Namca, but a third being, Huallallo Caruincho, defeated them and took control. He imposed strict rules on the people. Each woman was allowed to bear just two children and was forced to choose between them, keeping one to raise and giving up the other to be eaten by Huallallo Caruincho. The lands were rich and filled with perfect, brightly coloured parrots and toucans. Every seed that was planted ripened in five days. Similarly, when men or women died they returned to life after five days. But the people lived evil lives. Their easy life came to an end when Pariacaca emerged from the five eggs on Mount Condor Coto, and defeated Huallallo Caruincho. In Francisco de Avila's gloss on the legends (see main text) he comments that the lush lands were named Yunca or Ande, and that Yunca referred to the fertile valleys that lie towards the coast. In other versions they are called "anti lands", which scholars believe may have been a general term used to refer to warm lowland landscapes.

Working the dry soil of the continent's interior made life hard for many tribes. Myths recalling fruitful lands suggest that peoples such as the Huarochirí once lived in coastal valleys such as those near Paracas, shown here.

A Temple Made of Gold

Tiahuanaco – which lies near the southern end of Lake Titicaca, on the Callao plateau of Peru and Bolivia – is a stirring sight even today with its ruins of temples and palaces and its striking stone statues. At the height of the city's glory in the seventh century – with sunlight glittering on the temples' gold reliefs – it must have moved onlookers to awe.

The stonework of the Tiahuanaco temple was the finest found throughout the Andes until the coming of the Incas. The awe it inspired gave rise to tales of its legendary age.

Archaeologists believe that Tiahuanaco was home to some 50,000 people and the heart of an empire covering the southern and central Andes in the first millennium AD. At an altitude of more than 4000 metres, the size of the complex is truly remarkable. Why this civilization collapsed in around AD1000 remains a mystery, though some suggest that invaders overran it, others that the population starved or moved away following a long drought.

But when the Incas came to the Callao in the fifteenth century, they absorbed the local mythology, even declaring they were descended from the Tiahuanaco elite, their creator god emerging from sacred islands of Lake Titicaca.

Lost in the Dark

The Callao tell of a race of giants who lived in a time of darkness. A tall man named Con Ticci emerged from an island in Lake Titicaca with a group of followers and settled in Tiahuanaco, where he created the sun and moon. In some versions, the sun itself emerged from the lake and Con Ticci, who became the Inca god Viracocha, appeared from the south.

The giants angered Con Ticci and he turned them into rocks. Then at Tiahuanaco he carved statues representing a whole new race of Indians, the ancestors of those alive today. He made statues of all types of people and painted them in the colours and style of clothes they would wear. Then he told his followers to distribute these statues through forests, caves, mountains and rivers. When all the statues were in their place, Con Ticci commanded them to come to him – and the stone prototypes came to life. This is why the area's various communities have always dressed in different costumes.

Some say the Tiahuanaco statues were made in honour of the creator god by the first people, others that they were the giants that Con Ticci turned to stone in his rage. Others still maintain they were the people of a village who would not interrupt their dancing, drinking and festivities when the god came upon them on his travels.

Con Ticci taught people and healed the sick throughout the land, punishing those who tried to cross him, rewarding those who impressed. Wherever he performed great deeds, people built shrines in his honour. He travelled all his life until, at last, he left the land – where to no one knows.

Food of the Gods

Some say Indians from Tiahuanaco were responsible for discovering the coca plant, the leaves of which the peoples of the Andes have chewed for centuries. It is said to help alleviate the effects of living at high altitude.

Coca was revered. The leaves were sacrificed to gods and used for divination. Many myths explain its discovery.

It is said that the Indians of Tiahuanaco one day journeyed beyond the mountains. When they discovered lush valleys they settled there, burning the vegetation to clear the land so they could plant crops. But the smoke annoyed Khuno, god of snows, who whipped up a storm that forced the travellers to seek the shelter of mountain caves.

The storm destroyed all they had. But when hunger drove one man to taste the leaves of a green bush that seemed to grow all around, he felt new energy. He shared the leaves with the others and, invigorated, they returned to Tiahuanaco where they planted coca bushes in abundance.

One story tell how the coca bush grew from the body of a woman who had been killed for breaking the hearts of her many lovers. Another tells how a mother lost her child and wandered the land in grief. She came across a coca bush and found its leaves could ease her terrible pain.

Some Indians talk of coca as "our mother's fragrance" and link its origin with women. This Nazca pottery figure depicts a seated woman, chewing the sacred coca leaves.

Warriors of the South

The Araucanian Indians of Chile were fierce warriors. They succeeded in holding the Incas – and for a long time the Spanish – at bay by joining forces with other local tribes in times of war. They believed that the relations between their gods followed a similar pattern – but all the lesser deities were subject to Pillan, god of thunder and earthquakes.

The Indians of Chile, like the Peruvian Huarochirí (see page 40), looked back with terror to a time of darkness. In Araucanian mythology, the sun's light went out because two twins – Konkel and Pediu – stole it and shut it up in a jar. The birds could fly around in the dark atmosphere, but they could not find any food and as they grew hungrier they became more and more desperate, pleading with the brothers to set the light in the sky once more. In the end they offered to provide beautiful women for the twins if they would only free the sun, but Konkel and Pediu still refused. But at last, the partridge managed to knock the jar over, the sun was let loose and light returned to the world.

A Quarrel between Snakes

The Araucanians also had their own version of the flood myth told by Chibcha and Cañari Indians (see pages 28 and 34). Two snakes, Caicai and Tenten, fell into a quarrel one day, each claiming to have stronger powers of magic than the other. So they challenged each other to a contest. Caicai made the sea rise, while Tenten took the three-peaked mountain named Thegtheg ("Thundering" or "Glittering") and made it taller and taller to escape the floods. A few Indians, seeing the flood come, fled to Thegtheg and survived. In another version, the flood followed a volcanic eruption and earthquake. Traditionally, when there was an earthquake the Indians fled to Thegtheg, fearing another great flood.

The sender of earthquakes and other natural disasters was Pillan, the god of thunder, fire and volcanoes, and the Araucanians performed elaborate rituals to appease him. A host of other gods served Pillan: evil spirits named *guecufu*, which were to be found everywhere, bringing illness and spoiling the harvest; the shooting stars and comets, seen as evil omens; a fire creature with seven heads named

A fierce killer whale clutches a knife in its human hand. The orca appears in ceramics as far back as the Paracas culture, 800BC–AD1. This example is from the Nazca tribe, further up the western coast, and dates from the first millennium AD.

Dark Menagerie

Grotesque hybrid creatures and monsters that preyed on innocent souls filled the Araucanians' colourful mythology.

The *camahueto* was a vast seahorse which would cause shipwrecks, while the *cuero,* a clawed octopus, would feast on any man or animal foolish enough to enter the water. Sometimes it would come ashore to enjoy the sun's warmth, and then create storms to blow itself back out to sea. The *neguruvilu,* or *guirivilo,* was a fox crossed with a snake which emerged from its riverbed lair to catch its prey and dine on its blood. Then there was the *huallepen,* a sheep with a calf's head that lived in pools and streams; if it appeared to a pregnant woman, she would bear a deformed child. The *colocolo* was a small creature with poisonous saliva that lived in caverns underground. The *alicanto* was a bird that ate gold which made it shine brilliantly. When hunted, it could hide this light and in the dark it would lead people to their deaths high in the mountains. Perhaps most terrifying of all, however, was the hideous *chon-chon.* This fearsome creature was a bodiless human head that used its ears as wings and came by night to houses where people were sick. The legends told how it would fight sick people's souls, and, if it won, suck their blood.

Ihuaivilu, who lived in volcanoes; and Mueler, the lizard god of the whirlwind, whose help the Indians invoked to drive away evil spirits.

Living in close proximity to the ocean, particularly in the southern parts of their lands, the Araucanians told many tales of sea and river beasts. They even had their own version of the familiar mermaid legend.

As they told the story, a young woman was caring for her elderly mother who was ill. While she sat by her mother's side, she would gaze out of the window across the sun-drenched fields, towards the river. She longed to escape the dark worry of the house and go to bathe in the cool waters. But her mother did not want to be left alone, and told her daughter that she must stay by her bedside. They quarrelled, and the argument grew so heated that the young woman slapped her mother across the cheek – and in that instant the river rose, sweeping the faithless daughter away. The distraught mother hurried along the course of the river searching for her child and when eventually she came to the coast she met some fishermen who told her that they had seen a bizarre monster, half-fish, half-woman, being carried out to sea on the tide.

In later times, when fishermen saw the Sirena they pulled in their nets because they knew that fish disappeared when she was in the waters. Some myths told that people who saw the Sirena were doomed, like her, to die young. Sometimes she did not appear as a monster at all, but took the form of a beautiful young woman who was glimpsed either in mid-river or far out in a lake, standing on the water and combing her long, luxuriant hair in front of a mirror.

Land of Fire and Ice

At the southern end of South America lie the vast grasslands of Patagonia and the archipelagos of Tierra del Fuego. Right into this century Indians in these regions followed an ancient, mainly nomadic way of life, and their mythology and religious beliefs, almost untouched by the cultures of the Incas and of the Spanish invaders, can be seen as an echo – across the millennia – of the beliefs of the first migrating peoples who reached the continent in around 30,000BC.

The Yaghan, Alakaluf and Ona Indians of Tierra del Fuego shared a belief in a supreme being. A Yaghan Indian would pray to Watauineiwa ("the Most Ancient One") as "my father" and believed that the god – who had no need of a body – lived beyond the stars. Filled with goodness, he was the source of moral laws. The Ona believed in Temaukel, a similar supreme spirit god, without children or a wife, whose abode was beyond the heavens and who would listen to prayers from individual Indians. They believed that souls went to be with Temaukel at death. The Alakaluf, likewise, held that souls came from their supreme god, Xolas, at birth and returned to him after death.

According to the Ona, the world began in chaos until Temaukel sent Kenos, the ancestor of mankind, to establish order there. Kenos took two lumps of peat and fashioned them into male and female sexual organs. Their union created the first Ona Indians. Kenos lived among them and taught them how to speak and how to live together

peaceably. He then instructed two Ona brothers to carry on his teaching, and flew off into the night, settling in the sky as a sweep of stars.

But once Kenos was gone the brothers changed the rules he had established. Men and women could no longer rise full of strength after a short nap. And death also came into the world. When Kenos was still on Earth, Ona Indians who grew tired in old age went to sleep and when they awoke asked Kenos to wash them. After being bathed they began a new life all over again.

The brothers taught the men and women how to hunt seals, make fish oil, set fires and use tools – but then they began to quarrel. The elder brother believed it was too hard for men to find enough food and proposed that it should simply be provided. But his younger brother persuaded him that the harder it is to find something the more pleasure it brings.

Many years later, a great hunter named Kwanyip lived among the Ona. At that time, a black giant wandered the hills, preying on the people and spreading terror through the land. Kwanyip decided enough was enough and one day he set off alone to find him. Using all his cunning as a hunter he tracked the giant cannibal for several days and nights, and then attacked and killed him after a desperate struggle. When he returned to his people he was welcomed as a hero. Later he attacked and defeated Chenuke, the spirit of evil itself.

In some versions of the Kwanyip myth, the giant was invisible like the man in a story told by the Alakaluf Indians. Their Taquatu, though, was benign. He roamed the wilds unseen in his canoe and if he came across any Indians idling or day-dreaming, he would pick them up in his boat and take them away, dropping them off again in another place, many kilometres from home.

The unforgiving lands of the far south were slow to give up their secrets to the waves of invaders that swept the continent's more northern climes. In the Tierra del Fuego region of southern Chile, the mountains stood free from European influence for centuries after the coming of the conquistadors.

Pampas Legends

The Indians of the vast Patagonian pampas believed, like their fellows in Tierra del Fuego (see main text), in an invisible supreme god who lived beyond the world. But they also lived in fear of an evil deity named Balichu and a host of terrible demons, the Quezubû.

The hero El-lal almost died in his infancy. His father Nosthej, burning with hunger, was about to eat him when a rat scurried up and carried the tiny El-lal away. The rat raised El-lal and taught him about the plants of the Earth and the paths of the mountains. When he had grown into a youth, El-lal himself devised the bow and arrow and sling and began to hunt. His father caught up with him and El-lal, forgiving the old man, shared the secrets of hunting with him. Nosthej settled with El-lal in a mountain cave, but soon he was again overcome with the desire to eat his son. El-lal escaped and father chased son for miles and miles through the mountains. But just as Nosthej was about to grab hold of his quarry, a vast forest sprang up between them.

El-lal travelled on alone to the plains, where he found a race of men and women. They told him of a terrible giant, Goshy-e, that would capture and eat their children. El-lal found Goshy-e and attacked him, but the monster's hide was so tough that his arrows bounced off and landed in the ocean. So El-lal killed the monster by turning himself into a horsefly and stinging his belly.

After this triumph, El-lal resolved to marry and live among the people. He desired the daughter of the sun but, thinking herself superior, she rejected him. El-lal then looked around. The people had spread from the plains to the mountains and were using fire and hunting weapons as he had taught them. Seeing that his work was done, he resolved to depart the Earth. A beautiful swan appeared and carried him across the ocean to the east, where a lush island had risen from the sea at the place where El-lal's arrows had fallen into the waves.

CREATURES OF THE IMAGINATION

While the pre-Christian peoples of the Andes left no written records of their lifestyle and beliefs, they did leave vivid images of their imaginative landscape on their pottery and textiles. The exact significance of many of the pieces remains elusive, although the recurrence of animal figures, both wild and anthropomorphic, reflects a consciousness closely allied with the natural world. While certain mountains, rivers or caves were seen as sacred, so various creatures were believed to be mediators between the spheres of land, sea and air. They were embodiments of the cultural ideals of wisdom or ferocity, the totems of shamanic command; and they were also symbols of a culture's dominion over the world of the beasts and other men.

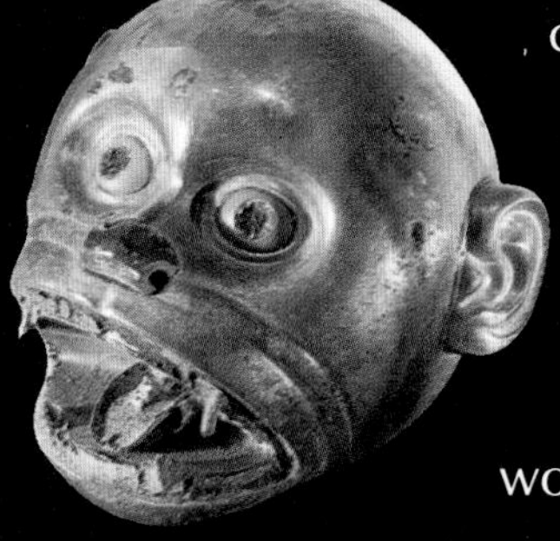

Above: This elaborate gold monkey-head, inlaid with the sacred materials turquoise and lapis, c.AD100–600, is shown with its tongue hanging out, an indication of ritual sacrifice. Such sacred images were often buried with Moche nobles.

The cat was a symbol of authority, seen as both protector and aggressor. The feline on the Nazca polychrome pottery bottle _(right)_ is shown with fruit, perhaps suggesting the pampas cat which had beneficial associations with vegetation as it inhabited fields, protecting crops by feeding on insects, birds and snakes. The vessel _(below)_, however, merges the feline form with that of the snake, producing an image of both spiritual power and physical might.

Above: The birds on this pre-Columbian textile recall the ancient divinity known as the Oculate Being (see pages 12–13). Some peoples also venerated birds by impersonating them, assuming plumage as part of tribal ritual.

Right: A deer assumes the same supplicant pose as a warrior captured in battle. Naked, a rope around its neck, its tongue has dropped out of its mouth, suggesting the Moche belief in the blood sacrifice of the adversary, whether man or beast.

EMPIRE OF THE SUN

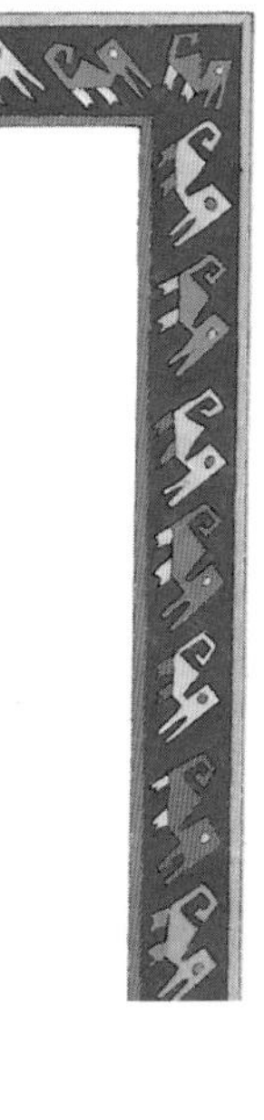

Meteorlike, the Inca empire lit up the sky of South American civilization for a brief but spectacular moment before it was brutally and unexpectedly extinguished. It arrived with little warning. For barely two centuries before their rise to power the Incas themselves were a relatively insignificant ethnic group, one among dozens of similar, competing tribes. And after a moment of glory that lasted little more than a hundred years, their realm was crushed by foreign invaders.

The difficulties in reconstructing the Incas's views are compounded by the fact that they had no writing with which to record them. Although they developed an ingenious record-keeping system involving knotted cords called *quipus*, the colour-coded threads and carefully positioned fastenings that it employed were hopelessly inadequate for detailing religious beliefs or handing on legends. Consequently, virtually everything that is now known about Inca mythology has come down through non-Inca sources, often in the writings of Spanish churchmen who, through their dedication to rooting out heathenism, were necessarily hostile witnesses.

Given all the handicaps, it is hardly surprising that the stories that have survived are incomplete and sometimes contradictory. The Incas themselves seem to have put more of their energy into the pragmatic world of war and government than into that of the imagination, and they were content to take much of their explanation of the universe from other Andean peoples. With the exception of the legends they passed on about their own early history, specifically Inca myths are few and far between.

Even so, the study of their customs and beliefs has unexpected rewards to offer. Rediscovering their mindset takes the observer into a bizarre world full of oddly distorted perspectives – a place in which people turn to stone and boulders come alive, where prayers are addressed to mountains and the dead pay social visits. Yet in other respects the religion of the Incas, with its customs of confession and penance, its tales of a universal flood and a long-robed redeemer, seems almost to portend the Christianity that was eventually to replace it. Today, after centuries of silence, the voices of the Incas can still reveal some surprising secrets.

Above, left: **The leather *quipu* was used as an *aide-memoire* by Inca bureaucrats and couriers. *Quipus* were light and portable, so messengers carried them easily around the empire.**

Opposite: **This elaborately-clad Inca warrior decorates the side of a wooden *kero* or ritual drinking vessel.**

Shamans and Sacred Stones

The roots of the religion of the Incas lay in a reverence for the living world and natural objects and in a belief that – whether for good or evil – some people had power to influence the spirit realm.

When Spanish missionaries first arrived in Peru, they quickly learned that objects called *huacas* were the focus of special devotion. From the start they had problems with the word, for the idea it represented had no exact Christian parallel. Most often they translated it as "idols", for many of the *huacas* were cult-objects fashioned from wood or stone. Sometimes "shrine" seemed more appropriate, for the term also encompassed holy sites.

But the concept stretched much further than either of those European notions. The chronicler Garcilaso de la Vega, himself half-Inca, caught the full animist flavour when he wrote of people worshipping plants, flowers, trees, mountains, rocks, caves, precious stones, wild animals and some species of birds. A *huaca* could be anything that incited religious wonder. For the Andean peoples the natural world was alive with spiritual power.

The great temple of Sacsahuaman outside the city of Cuzco shows Inca stonework at its finest. Each block was individually cut to fit its neighbours. No mortar was used. When earthquakes, which shook the region regularly, struck, the stones simply shifted and then moved back into position.

This Inca doll, wrapped in a colourful wool blanket, was probably never a plaything. It was found in a tomb and most likely had some sacred significance.

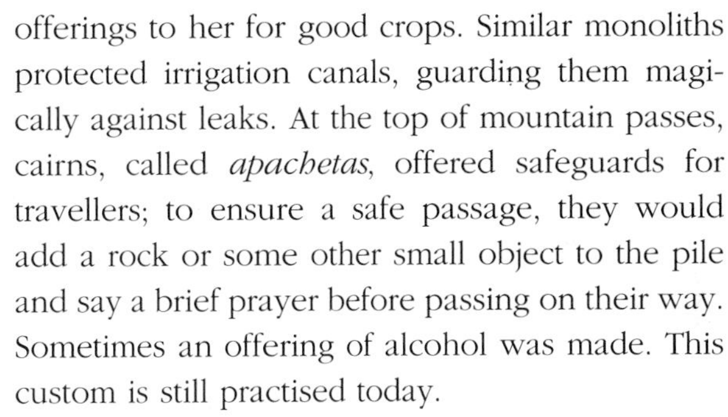

Some features attracted particular veneration. Mountains were especially revered. Other focuses of devotion were large or oddly-shaped stones.

The *huacas* had their parallels in Inca mythology. Tales of the dynasty's founder, Manco Capac, told how at the end of his life he was turned into stone, a fate also supposed to have befallen his brothers (see page 66) and the first race of humans. Sometimes the process happened in reverse. In the battle that saw the great emperor Pachacuti drive Chanca invaders back from the walls of Cuzco, the boulders on the hills above the city were said to have been transformed into warriors who turned the tide of the fight. Later, Pachacuti spread the word that they were gods who put on flesh to help him as a secret weapon in all his subsequent campaigns.

On a humbler level, farmers set standing stones in the middle of fields in honour of the Earth goddess, Pachamama, and would make offerings to her for good crops. Similar monoliths protected irrigation canals, guarding them magically against leaks. At the top of mountain passes, cairns, called *apachetas*, offered safeguards for travellers; to ensure a safe passage, they would add a rock or some other small object to the pile and say a brief prayer before passing on their way. Sometimes an offering of alcohol was made. This custom is still practised today.

Huacas could also take the form of personal talismans, often in the shape of pebbles carved to resemble llamas, ears of maize or tiny human beings. In the home, too, there would most likely be some small object, wrapped in cloth or displayed in a niche. Sometimes the house would have another, odder guardian, for the Andean peoples combined ancestor worship with their veneration of the natural world. Archaeological discoveries over the past hundred years have revealed that the practice of mummifying the dead stretched back perhaps as much as five thousand years before the coming of the Incas, and it continued under their rule. Often, the process was left to nature; corpses were simply taken out to the

This 23-cm-high silver llama wears a royal blanket decorated in gold and cinnabar. No one knows the exact purpose of objects such as this but it has been suggested that they may have been either toys or little household *huacas*. The Inca calendar was punctuated with sacrifices of llamas.

high mountains or to the coastal desert to dry out. More exalted individuals were treated by artificial techniques. Families would sometimes keep the preserved bodies of a deceased father or mother in the house, treating them with deference and parading them through the streets dressed in fine clothes on the occasion of the annual Festival of the Dead.

No one carried respect for their ancestors to greater lengths than the Inca ruling house. In Peru it was customary for the dead to retain their personal possessions, which were normally either buried with them or in places they had loved. In the case of royal mummies, that meant keeping their own palaces; their heirs were expected to build themselves new ones. There the preserved corpses would sit in state, cared for by clan groups known as *panacas*. Vast estates were put at the *panacas'* disposal so they could keep the dead kings – and themselves also – in the state to which they were accustomed. To maintain the illusion that normal life continued, the mummies would pay social calls on one another, and on important ceremonial occasions would be brought out to attend the festivities in Cuzco's main square.

Ancestral Centres of Worship

Another form of ancestor worship was the respect paid to *paccariscas* – the places where tribal ancestors were believed to have emerged into the upper world (see page 64). These could be caves, hills, lakes or springs, and they became important centres for public thanksgiving.

Nowhere had as many as Cuzco itself, where the Incas feted their own origins. Early in the seventeenth century, a Spanish priest called Bernabé Cobo took it upon himself to find out all that he could about these local sanctuaries. In his *History of the New World*, Cobo listed no fewer than 350 shrines within a radius of 33 kilometres around the old Inca capital, ranging from rocks and springs to battlefields. He reported that local people conceived of them as radiating out in spokes from the city's great sun temple, the Coricancha. There were 41 of these lines and each one was the responsibility of a clan, that was expected to tend the shrines in their care and offer sacrifices on appropriate occasions.

According to Cobo, the attendants to whom the duties were delegated were usually old people past more active work. When questioned, they would explain the significance of their particular *huaca*, acting as a kind of oral memory-bank. They knew the correct formulas for making sacrifices and the offerings that were to be given, and would promise prospective worshippers, in Cobo's words, "high hopes of good luck, listing previous successes to boost the reputation of the shrine".

Even when Cobo was drawing up his catalogue he had to rely on the memory of his informants to identify the *huacas*, for most had disappeared. Generations of priests before him had made it their business to remove what they saw as relics of idolatry. Many boasted of their successes, and the numbers they quote give some idea of the sheer quantity of the objects that the Indians held sacred. One missionary, for example, recorded that he had personally destroyed more than 30,000 "idols" and some 3000 mummies during his career.

Among the first objects of the Spaniards' attentions were the oracles: holy sites to which rulers and commoners alike would go for advice

The Stone that Wept

A legend of Cuzco told of a massive boulder outside the city walls that wept tears of blood. Behind the tale lay memories of a real-life tragedy that marred the construction of one of the Incas' greatest architectural achievements.

Made of massive blocks of masonry, many of them weighing more than a hundred tonnes, the fortress of Sacsahuaman overlooking Cuzco startled the conquistadors with its Cyclopean bulk, leading some to call it the eighth wonder of the world. But one of the largest boulders intended for its construction never reached the site. Instead it remained on the plateau in front of the fortress, so exhausted by its long journey from the mines, the Cuzcans claimed, that it had come to rest and wept blood.

The truth, according to Garcilaso de la Vega, was that the stone had been deliberately left by the Indians who pulled it there. They abandoned it following a disaster that occurred in the course of the journey, when the huge stone broke loose on a mountain road, crushing many of those who were dragging it. In the chronicler's words, it was these victims – he puts their number at an improbable three thousand – who wept tears of blood, and the stone remained isolated and unused outside the capital as their monument.

on important questions or to learn what the future had in store. In a world in which natural features were frequently imbued with numinous powers, oracles were commonly in the open air.

But the greatest of all the Andean oracles lay at Pachacamac, not far from modern-day Lima. Its reputation long pre-dated the Incas, who did not dare to tamper with it when they conquered the region in the late fifteenth century. Instead they contented themselves with building the largest sun temple in the kingdom next to it and with identifying its presiding deity, the eponymous Pachacamac, with their own god Viracocha.

In its heyday, people came from all parts of Peru as well as from southern Ecuador to consult the oracle, which was located in a chamber atop a stepped adobe-brick pyramid. The god who resided there not only offered advice to individuals, including the Inca himself, but was also reputedly able to provide protection against bad weather, crop failure, earthquakes and disease.

In return he expected tribute. Offerings in the shape of cotton, maize, dried fish, textiles and gold poured in, but they were not enough to satisfy the divinity, who also required the blood of sacrificial victims. Hecatombs of llamas and guinea-pigs were slaughtered to feed the idol, and in earlier times there were human victims, too, to judge from the mummies of women showing signs of strangulation that the archaeologist Max Uhle found on the site in 1897.

Presumably the officials in charge of the oracle had, like their counterparts at Delphi in ancient Greece, a good grasp of politics that enabled them under normal circumstances to give appropriate advice. Yet they were far from infallible. When the conquistadors were holding the Inca Atahualpa as a prisoner, he received a visit from the priests of Pachacamac. His captors were surprised to see that he treated them with contempt, even suggesting to the Spaniards that they should put them in chains and let them see if their god could arrange their release. Asked to explain his hostility, he replied that the oracle was false, for on three crucial questions it had given bad advice. It had predicted that his father Huayna Capac would recover from his final illness if taken out into the sunlight, whereas in fact he had died; it had told Huascar, Atahualpa's rival for the throne, that he would succeed in the civil war that divided the two, but in reality he had lost; and it had advised Atahualpa himself to attack the Spanish invaders, assuring him that he would kill them all.

Despite such failures, the Andean peoples had a passion for divination that was not satisfied by the oracles alone. Soothsaying and promises of good luck were the principal stock-in-trade of the shamans who flourished in all parts of the Inca lands. Although they had low social standing, they were consulted even by the nobility, and their advice was invariably sought before any major decision was taken. On a humbler level, local people turned to them whenever they wished to find lost objects or learn news of absent friends.

The diviners used a bewildering variety of techniques to predict the future. Some gazed at the ashes of charcoal fires; others studied cobwebs or interpreted dreams. The *calparicu* – literally, "those who bring good fortune" – inflated the lungs of sacrificial birds or animals and scrutinized them for signs of what the future would bring. There were practitioners, too, who cast lots with ears of maize, beans or pebbles; who studied the

This lovely silver maize cob dates from AD1430–1532. It was probably used as an offering. The palace of the Inca ruler had a whole garden of life-size, golden animals and plants similar to this one.

movement of giant spiders kept in tightly lidded jars; or who simply observed the flow of saliva spat into the palm of their hand.

Other, more sinister activities might also be involved, for among the ranks of the shamans were many sorcerers who practised black magic in secret and whose malign influence was widely feared. They were associated with spiders, lizards, snakes, toads and moths, and it was bad luck to see any of these creatures near someone's home. Even the Inca king feared enchantment; women attendants instantly swallowed any hairs that fell from his head lest they should fall into the hands of hostile shamans.

Such practices were the downside of a world-view that contained much superstition but was also full of devoutness and wonder. Without a written faith or creed, the Incas saw divinity all about them and humbly acknowledged their own limited place in the natural world. Constantly chastened by life's menacing unpredictability, they moved respectfully and fearfully through a world of ever-present spirits.

On one side of this ritual drinking vessel, Incas bear sacks of offerings. On the other is a carved head. The vessel dates from around AD1500.

Atonement for Sins and Misdemeanours

When Spanish priests first arrived in Peru, they were startled to find that the Andean peoples had their own rites of confession and were already used to the idea of doing penance for their sins.

Confessions were usually made to the priestly attendants, male or female, responsible for the upkeep of shrines. The worst sins were murder, theft, sacrilege or treason; in contrast, adultery and fornication were regarded merely as misdemeanours. If the confessor felt that the penitent was telling less than the whole truth, he or she might resort to divination to settle the issue and would use a stone to pummel the bent back of anyone considered to be lying.

Penances were apt to be severe, "especially if the man who had committed the sin was poor and could not give anything to the confessor", as one Christian commentator sourly noted. They almost always involved fasting, which in Inca terms did not mean going without food altogether but merely without meat and seasonings. A more peculiar punishment involved being beaten with nettles by hunchbacks who had been specially employed for this purpose.

Any misfortune was taken as a sure sign of transgression, and when harm came to the Inca ruler the whole nation did penance. Even the ruler himself and his family were expected to participate. But they confessed their faults in secret to their father Inti, for it was not considered fitting for the Children of the Sun to reveal their weaknesses to any human intermediary.

Instructor of the World

Long before the coming of Christianity, the Incas and their Andean neighbours believed in a supreme creator god. They gave him many titles, among them Ilya Ticci Viracocha Pacayacacic – "Age-Old Creator Lord, Instructor of the World".

Many decades after the empire fell, the Incas still remembered a tale about their greatest ruler, the empire-builder Pachacuti. They told how, as a young man, he was on his way to visit his father, the reigning Inca, when he came to a spring called Susur-pugaio. As he passed, a flash of light caught his eye, and when he looked into the water he saw that a piece of crystal had fallen into it. Gazing intently at the glassy nugget, he was amazed to spot inside it a tiny figure with three bright rays like those of the sun radiating from its head. The apparition wore Inca-style ear-pieces and dress, and on its forehead was the *llautu*, a scarlet head-band that was the Inca symbol of royalty. Yet the figure's kingship was obviously beyond the human realm, for serpents coiled around its arms, and Pachacuti could see lions' heads over its shoulders and between its legs.

The creator deity Viracocha was venerated by many tribes in the Andes. This stele, dated AD600–1200, is from Tiahuanaco, a city abandoned by the time of the Incas.

Terrified by the sight, the future ruler took to his heels, only to be summoned back by a commanding voice. The figure told him not to fear, for he was Viracocha, the creator lord. He informed Pachacuti that he would conquer many nations, but must take care to honour his divine protector and remember him in his sacrifices. The vision then vanished, though the crystal remained. Pachacuti kept it and was said to be able to look into it and see the regions he would later subdue.

Pachacuti was so impressed by the apparition that he later had a golden statue prepared to his instructions to capture its appearance. The image was that of a bearded man – unusually, for the Incas themselves were clean-shaven. It was placed in Viracocha's temple in Cuzco, and was said to be about the size of a ten-year-old boy.

The god whom Pachacuti had been privileged to glimpse was acknowledged by all the peoples of the southern Andes as the creator of the universe. Although the details of the creation story often varied in the telling, all agreed in setting the events in the Callao region around Lake Titicaca and in the ancient, ruined city of Tiahuanaco nearby, which had been abandoned centuries before the Incas rose to prominence. Also common to each version of the story was a belief in an earlier race of beings that had been swept away in a cataclysmic flood.

In essence, the story told how Viracocha fashioned the Earth and sky in darkness, then set the sun and the moon in the heavens to give them light. He made humankind in his own image, first creating a generation of giants to inhabit the newly-established world. But the giants displeased him, and he punished some by turning them to stone – a tale that apparently served to explain the presence of huge stone statues at Tiahuanaco, some of which are still there to this day. The rest of the giants were swept away in the deluge that then inundated the Earth.

Her Majesty the Moon

In the Andean scheme of things most gods, except the creator Viracocha, were paired off with female counterparts, and the sun and moon made an obvious couple. Mama Kilya – Mother Moon – occupied a special place in the Inca pantheon. As consort of the sun god Inti, she was the maternal ancestor of the royal line.

As Inti's partner, Mama Kilya had her own shrine in Cuzco's great Coricancha temple. It was decorated with sheets of beaten silver and served by its own priestesses. Considered the ruling Inca's mother just as the sun was his father, she was also identified with the Coya or the Inca's principal wife.

Throughout the Andes region, lunar eclipses were regarded with terror, for it was thought that some monstrous creature was trying to devour the moon. To scare the attacker away, people brandished weapons at the heavens and made all the noise they were capable of, even whipping their dogs to make them bark.

Although Mama Kilya was a revered figure, her position was not high enough for some of the peoples the Incas conquered. In particular, the Chimu of Ecuador, who had long venerated the moon as their principal deity, were less than pleased when she was forced to take on a secondary role. But Inca might prevailed, and the Chimu too had to adjust their pantheon to give pride of place to the imperial Inti. This was despite the fact that they had traditionally regarded the sun as a hostile power.

This pottery figure, which dates from the Inca period, wears a ceremonial half-moon pendant. He or she carries several drinking vessels and may be performing some kind of ritual.

In a second act of creation Viracocha then reappeared on Earth, some said at Tiahuanaco and others at Lake Titicaca, either from the waters or on an island that later became the seat of a great temple. He caused the sun and moon, whose light had been dimmed, to shine once more, and they cast their first light from the mountains that backed the lake. It was then that he created all the different peoples of the Earth, giving them their distinctive dress and customs (see box opposite).

Lord of Divination and the Seasons

Viracocha was widely venerated in the Inca world as the universal creator and master of all. Prayers addressed to him called him the Lord of Divination and the Seasons, omnipresent and omnipotent, able to grant the gift of life itself. When he was invoked in the company of other gods, his name always came first. Yet, for all that, he remained a remote and insubstantial figure. Although the Incas built temples to him, including a splendid one in Cuzco, he was overshadowed in terms of public ceremonial by other gods. No great estates were assigned to the upkeep of his places of worship as they were for other deities – an omission the Incas justified by claiming that, as he was the creator of everything, he had need of nothing.

Insofar as this faceless divinity eventually came to acquire a personality, it was through his identification with a separate figure of Callao legend, Thunupa (see pages 94–95). Andean tales of this culture hero described how, like Viracocha, he arrived mysteriously from the south on the banks of Lake Titicaca at a time when the sun had just returned after a long absence. He had magical powers to make water flow from stone and the imprint of his feet could be seen even in hard rock. He, too, was described as a bearded man, dressed in a long tunic, and stories told how he

Tiahuanaco, which was established around AD200, was the highest city in the ancient world, and more than a thousand years later its ruins still awed the Incas. Huge monoliths such as this inspired legends about an ancient race of giants.

moved northwards through the Andean foothills inspiring universal veneration and acquiring the name of Ticci Viracocha, or Creator Lord.

Because of their beards and their mysterious appearance apparently out of nowhere, the Spanish conquistadors found themselves referred to as "Viracochas" among the native people when they first arrived. The illusion did not last long. No one expressed the disenchantment that replaced it better than the Inca Titu Cusi, one of the last Inca rulers. "I thought they were kindly beings sent (as they claimed) by Ticci Viracocha, that is to say by God," he told his fellow nobles. "But it seems to me that all has turned out the very opposite from what I believed. For let me tell you, brothers, from proofs they have given me since their arrival in our country, they are the sons not of Viracocha, but of the Devil." Seeing their land ravaged and their people abused, few of his audience would have disagreed.

Why People Dress Differently

According to one myth, all the diverse Andean races could trace their origins back to the repopulation of the Earth after the flood, when the creator god fashioned them just as they were in Inca times.

The chronicler Cristobal de Molina was told that the creator god Viracocha made the different peoples out of clay, and then painted on the garments that each group were to wear. Each was given its own language, songs and favourite foodstuffs – even a preferred hairstyle, long or short.

Then the creator sent them underground to make their way to the various regions to which he had assigned them; the caves, lakes and mountains from which they re-emerged into the light would subsequently be worshipped as holy places. The first generation were in due course turned into stone, and they too subsequently became objects of reverence.

The purpose of the tale seems to have been to explain the different clothes and customs of the various Andean peoples at a time when each ethnic group was most easily marked out by their distinctive garb. Even today there are recognizable differences between the traditional dress of adjoining valleys, and profound respect continues to be shown to rocks and stones.

The Tavern of the Dawn

The stories the Incas told of their own origins were fragmentary and confused, littered with the shards of conflicting legends. The only constant features were a handful of sacred sites that in historic times were honoured with much royal pomp and ceremony.

When the American explorer Hiram Bingham came across the temple with three windows at Machu Picchu in 1911, he believed at first that he had found the Tavern of the Dawn. This would have made the ancient city the birthplace of the Inca race itself. In fact, subsequent scholars have decided that Machu Picchu was a late construction, built in the last years of the Inca empire. Building the city must have been an enormous undertaking, so the reason for its abandonment is still a mystery.

When the Spaniards asked the Inca inhabitants of Peru about their own origins, they received a variety of answers that almost never tallied in all their details. Such diversity was no doubt only to be expected in an oral culture with no written canon of myth. Yet certain places that played a part in Inca ceremonial constantly recurred in the stories, which were similar enough in their essentials to suggest a common source.

One shared element was the name of the founder of the dynasty. He was called Manco Capac, and his sister-wife was Mama Ocllo. Another was a place called Pacaritambo – literally, the Tavern of the Dawn – which has been identified with a cave twenty-five kilometres southwest of Cuzco.

One version of the myth has Manco and his wife emerging with two brothers and two sisters from one of three cavern entrances there; the ancestors of other, non-royal Inca clans reportedly came out of the mouths of the other caverns. Other informants called the place of origin Tambotocco, the Tavern of the Windows, now generally thought to be simply a variant of Pacaritambo. One source explained the name by recording that Manco Capac had built there "a masonry wall with three windows".

This statement caused the American explorer Hiram Bingham some excitement in 1911, when he discovered the city of Machu Picchu. Noting that the temple there had three openings in the wall – an unusual feature, as most of the Incas' big stone structures had none – he initially persuaded himself that he had found the dynasty's legendary first home. But now it is generally accepted that Machu Picchu was a relatively late foundation.

Hidden in a Cave

The notion that Manco and his siblings emerged from a cave echoed other Andean tales of *paccariscas* (see page 56). It also fitted in with the idea that Viracocha repopulated the Earth after the flood by sending the various races underground to their appointed homes (see page 62). Some similar idea evidently survived in Cobo's remark that "the Incas worshipped the cave of Pacaritambo as an important shrine because in that place their ancestors had escaped from the destruction of the world [in the flood]".

Other sources, however, told a very different tale, in which Manco and his wife made their first appearance at Lake Titicaca. According to Garcilaso de la Vega, the couple were set down by the sun god Inti on the shores of the lake and given a golden rod "a little shorter than a man's arm and two fingers thick". They were told to wander the land and to plunge the rod into the earth whenever they stopped to eat or sleep. At the spot where it disappeared entirely into the ground – indicating good, deep soil – they were to establish their court. That place turned out to be the Cuzco valley.

For all their differences, both versions agreed in ascribing a significant role in the Incas' wanderings to Huanacauri – literally, "Dry Mountain" – twelve kilometres from the future capital. In Garcilaso's account, it was there that the rod was finally swallowed up by the soil. (He also mentions Pacaritambo, but treats it merely as an inn at which the couple stopped on their wanderings.)

Lake Titicaca, at 3810m the highest lake in the world, was revered by the ancient peoples of the Andes. Many of them believed that their ancestors had either been put on Earth near the lake or had emerged from it.

The cave legends told a more complex and probably earlier tale of the sacred mountain. They spoke of Ayar Cachi, one of Manco's brothers, who had godlike powers to open up ravines and flatten hills with the boulders that he threw from his sling. His brothers soon tired of his strength and boastfulness, however, and decided to get rid of him. Enticing him into a cave, they blocked up the entrance and proceeded on their way. But Ayar Cachi magically escaped from his prison and caught up with them at a place called Tampoquiru. Having told them to make their capital in Cuzco, he proceeded to Huanacauri where he turned himself to stone. A second brother, Ayar Uchu, sprouted wings before suffering the same fate.

The presence of two *huacas* or sacred stones representing the brothers accounted for the hill's important role in subsequent Inca ritual. It was the home of the oldest of Cuzco's shrines, where the spindle-shaped boulder into which Ayar Uchu had supposedly been transformed was preserved and venerated. Here adolescents of an age to join the ranks of the Inca nobility were brought during the important annual festival of Capac Raymi. After spending a night at the foot of the mountain, they would climb up to the shrine to be presented with the war-slings that marked their entry into the ranks of the warrior-knights. The link thus forged between the young nobles and the sacred site was a strong and lasting one. When Atahualpa's chief of staff Chalcuchima was executed by the Spaniards, the names on which the brave old general called as he burned alive were Viracocha – the creator god – and Huanacauri.

Manco's Shining Mantle

The Spanish chroniclers liked to tell a story suggesting that the Incas' supposedly divine authority as sons of the sun in fact resulted from a simple deception. According to the Spanish propaganda, Manco Capac's clothing fooled the Indians, showing them to be credulous and their rulers to be ruthless and cynical.

To make his first entry into his future capital of Cuzco, the first Inca, Manco Capac, wore a cape of gold, so the tale goes – or, in an alternative version, two thin plaques of the metal on his chest and back.

He had sent messengers ahead to spread the news that the son of the sun himself was coming to town. According to the story, when the gullible citizens saw him parading in his supposed father's reflected glory, they instantly fell down and praised him as a god.

Although the Spaniards may purposely have put a cynical gloss on the story, there is evidence to suggest the rulers consciously played upon popular credulity to bolster their authority.

From Huanacauri the siblings proceeded to Cuzco itself. In some versions of the myth (see box) they were welcomed by the natives, who instantly recognized their divine authority. Other accounts told of battles fought before the Incas could establish themselves in their future capital.

How Manco's Sister Terrorized Cuzco

Perhaps the oddest legend described how the city first fell to one of Manco's sisters. Having slain one of its inhabitants somewhere in the surrounding countryside, she cut him open and removed his lungs – a practice that was usually associated with shamans, who used it on sacrificial animals. Entering the city with the blood-smeared organs in her mouth, she so terrified the citizens, who assumed that she was a cannibal, that they all fled, abandoning their former home to the newcomers.

Such stories have a primitive ring to them that suggests they may well date from early times. But in the absence of written records, it is now all but impossible to disentangle the historical basis from all the confusion of legend.

All that can be said with certainty is that the sites the Incas venerated as sacred to their ancestors were grouped in two particular areas, one in the Tiahuanaco-Lake Titicaca region and the other immediately around the capital, Cuzco. That dichotomy has led some scholars to suggest a dual origin, with migrants from the region around Titicaca merging with people from the immediate surroundings of Cuzco jointly to produce the mighty Inca race.

Before his execution in Cuzco in 1572, the last Inca, Tupac Amaru, made a speech from the scaffold to the largely Indian crowd assembled to watch. In it he told his listeners that the claims he and his forefathers had made of conversing with the sun were not true. He then explained that his brother and predecessor on the throne, Titu Cusi, had told him what to do when he needed to persuade his people of something. Titu Cusi said he was to go alone to the Punchao – the golden solar disc that was the Incas' holiest emblem – when he had an important message for his subjects. "Afterwards I was to come out and say that it had spoken to me, and that it said whatever I wished," he told the crowd, adding "But it did not speak, we alone did; for it is an object of gold and cannot speak."

It seems most likely that he made the speech under duress; the Spanish were not averse to torture after all. Or that Spanish chroniclers could have been casting the last Incas' farewell speech in a particularly bad light. But it is not too far-fetched to suppose that Tupac Amaru may have wished to warn his people against putting too much faith in the old ways, which were already being shown to fail them.

The Incas' first ancestor, Manco Capac, wears a golden chest-piece which reflects the glory of his father, the sun.

Children of the Sun

To the complexity of Andean religion with its myriad spirits and deities, the conqueror Pachacuti brought an imperial vision. One god would unite all his disparate realms, and that would be his own mythical father, Inti the sun.

As a young prince, Pachacuti was not his father's choice as heir to the throne. He attained royalty through a decisive action that set the tone for his subsequent career. At that time – early in the fifteenth century, when across the Atlantic Ocean the Renaissance was coming into flower – the Inca realm was small and insecure, and Cuzco itself was threatened by the warriors of the neighbouring Chanca people. In this crisis, the reigning Inca and his heir had sought refuge in the mountains. But Pachacuti was made of sterner stuff, and he resolved to defend the capital. He won a

Pachacuti encouraged the cult of one deity above all others. This was the sun god Inti, worshipped in the Andes since ancient times. This mask of the sun god dates from c.300BC.

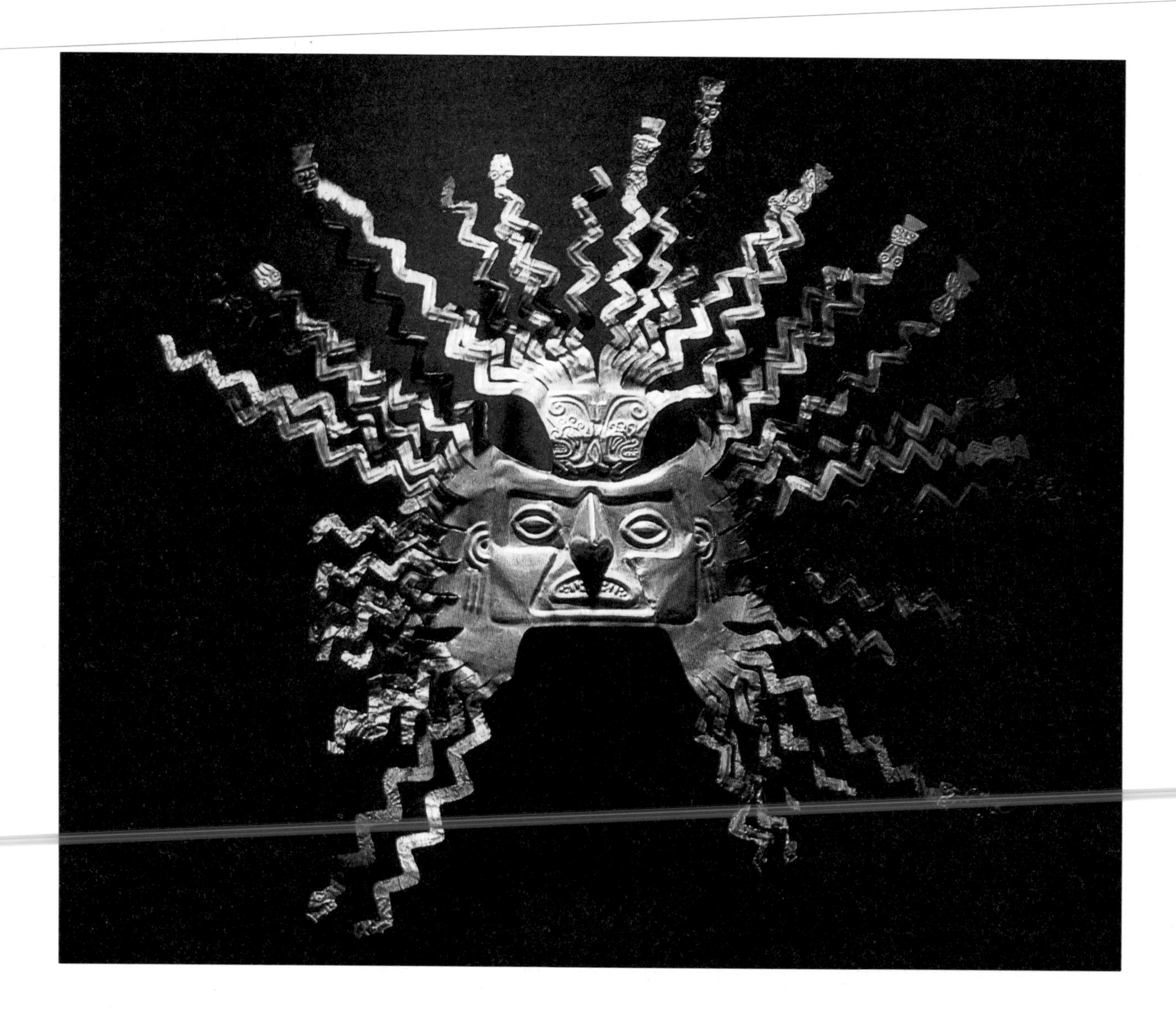

resounding victory, putting the foe to rout. In the wake of this triumph he forced his father to abdicate and established himself as the new monarch.

Yet his position remained insecure. He had many brothers whose claim to the throne was theoretically as good as his own. The influence of the Inca nobility – the people the Spaniards were to dub the *orejones* or "long ears" (see box) – was great. But Pachacuti had no desire to be merely the first among equals either within his realm or in the wider world of Andean politics, where many rival kingdoms competed for power. He rapidly set about establishing an absolute autocracy at home, while abroad he launched a series of campaigns that were to create the greatest empire South America had yet known.

The Chief God

Yet Pachacuti was not only a military leader; his imperial vision stretched to religious matters, too. In the divine sphere he sought to impose the worship of a single, focal god whose prestige on the celestial plane would echo and enhance his own worldly dominion. And like absolute monarchs in such lands as Egypt and Japan before him, the divinity with which Pachacuti chose to identify himself was the sun.

The worship of Inti, the sun god, was promulgated throughout the empire. In the Inca heartland the deity attained a pre-eminence he had not known before. Elsewhere his cult marched with Pachacuti's armies. As new provinces were conquered, their leaders were given the option of accepting Inti while continuing also to worship their old gods or else of facing annihilation. Not surprisingly, most proved amenable to the former.

Pachacuti lost no opportunity to stress his own links to the god. As the son of Inti, he was the sun's living representative on Earth. In that role he acted as mediator for the entire human race, interceding for its well-being with his heavenly father. The ruler took pains to make the link apparent in every possible way. Hardly a royal

The Noble Art of Ear-Piercing

The Inca aristocracy wore their status proudly in the shape of heavy golden earrings that stretched the lobes. The ornaments marked out the wearers instantly from their social inferiors and won them the disrespectful Spanish nickname of "long ears".

The piercing of the ears was the climax of a round of initiation ceremonies for adolescents between the ages of twelve and fifteen that took place at the annual festival of Capac Raymi, the most splendid in the Inca year. Noble families came to Cuzco from all over the empire to attend the festivities, which stretched through much of the month of November. Noble-born youths who were to be accepted into the knightly class attended a round of rituals, trials and sacrifices, including a race down a hill outside the city in which participants were occasionally seriously injured. Finally came the moment when their ears were pierced with a golden needle and a golden ear-spool was inserted. It was a severe blow if, at some future time, a knight's ear was torn in battle, for he could thereby be prevented from showing off the most distinctive mark of his nobility.

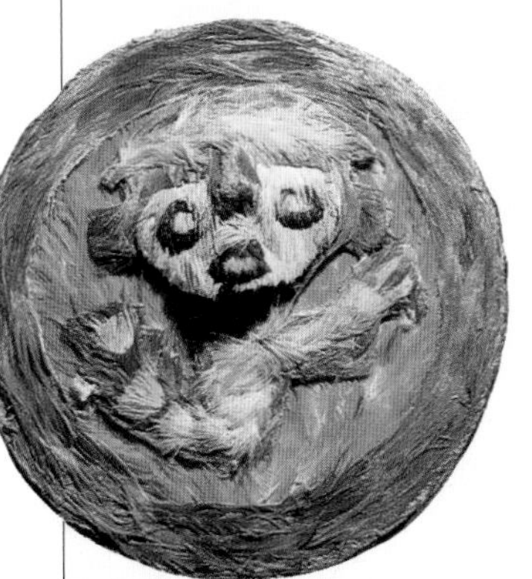

Brightly coloured feathers decorate these elaborate ear-spools. The green feathers are parrot, the yellow and red are macaw and the purple are from the honey creeper. These spools, from the Chimu culture, were probably made during the Inca period.

Pachacuti and the Girl from Ica

An Inca legend told how the dynasty's greatest ruler showed generosity to one of his subjects even when she rejected his advances.

As Pachacuti was travelling through the coastal province of Ica one day, his eye was caught by the beauty of a girl he saw working in the fields. Courtiers ran up to tell her that she had had the honour of winning the ruler's favour, but in spite of all their offers of costly gifts she turned down the prospect of dallying with the sun-king, saying that she loved another man.

The ruler's attendants expected him to punish her temerity, but instead he praised her constancy and offered to reward her, asking her to name the gift of her choice. Instead of demanding gold or jewels, she said only that she would like water for her village, which lay in an arid desert region. Pleased by her unselfishness, the Inca ordered 40,000 soldiers to dig irrigation canals to provide the community with a year-round supply – or so the story claimed, though actually the channels in the area predated the Incas by several hundred years.

Sixteenth-century Peruvian nobles worship the Inca Manco, who had been appointed by the Spaniards. The Incas continued to believe that their leader was a descendent of the sun god even when he was put to death by the conquistadors. This drawing is the work of Felipe Guaman Poma de Ayala; it dates from about 1565 and is taken from his *Chronicle of the New World.*

decree was issued that did not start by proclaiming the Inca's heavenly connection. The religious calendar was revised to exclude a number of non-Inca festivals, while others sacred to Inti were added. Sacrifices to the god were performed daily in Cuzco's main square, where a fire of specially carved wood was lit for the purpose at daybreak. It became customary, too, for ordinary citizens to blow a ritual kiss known as the *mocha* each dawn to the rising sun. Meanwhile, to stress the historical basis of the relationship, the mummies of the seven Inca rulers who had preceded Pachacuti were brought out daily to face the rising sun in mute homage to their divine parent.

Much of this ceremonial was dictated by reasons of state, for Pachacuti's own personal attitude to Inti remained equivocal. While making the sun god the focus of public worship, in private he mused over the deity's limitations; the sun could not be all-powerful, he claimed, for otherwise he would never allow mere clouds to obscure his face, and would sometimes take time to rest from his ceaseless journeying across the heavens. In consequence, Pachacuti took care to ensure that Inti never displaced Viracocha as the supreme deity. To complicate the picture further, Pachacuti himself seems to have recognized a personal allegiance to a third power, Illapa the thunder god, carrying a golden image of the deity with him whenever he went on campaign.

The Golden Temple

In public, however, Inti reigned supreme, and a massive programme of temple-building helped cement his cult. It was nowhere more apparent than in Cuzco itself, where Pachacuti created one of the world's most extraordinary religious edifices. The Coricancha, or House of Gold, was just that: a building made of monumental stone blocks overlaid with extraordinary quantities of the precious metal. A strip of gold two handspans wide ran all the way round the building's exterior, and the gateway and doors were panelled with gold. So was the interior of the chapel of Inti, the foremost of six that radiated from the temple's central courtyard; and on its far wall, positioned to catch the light of the rising sun, was the Punchao, a golden solar image in the form of a human face surrounded by rays.

When Cuzco was eventually won by the Spaniards, this treasure fell as booty to a soldier named Manso Serra, who subsequently lost it in the course of a night's gambling. His misadventure gave rise to a proverbial saying, "He'd lose the sun before it rises", used to describe a wastrel.

Few Spaniards ever saw the Coricancha in all its splendour, for it was stripped of its treasures by Pizarro's men in the course of the conquest. Those

A Heritage of Craftsmanship

Like absolute monarchs before and since, the Incas sought to justify their ascendancy by painting a bleak picture of the life their subjects led before they enjoyed the benefits of Inca rule.

Twenty-five years after the Spanish conquest, the chronicler Garcilaso de la Vega asked his uncle, a survivor of the Inca royal line, to tell him about his people's origins. The old man started by describing the condition of the Andean peoples before they came under imperial Inca rule. They lived like wild beasts, he claimed, without religion, government, agriculture or even clothes. Their homes were caves or crannies in the rocks, their food berries, roots and sometimes human flesh. Even their sex lives were primitive, for "they knew nothing of having separate wives". This miserable existence caused the sun to take pity on humankind and to send the Inca to teach them civilized ways.

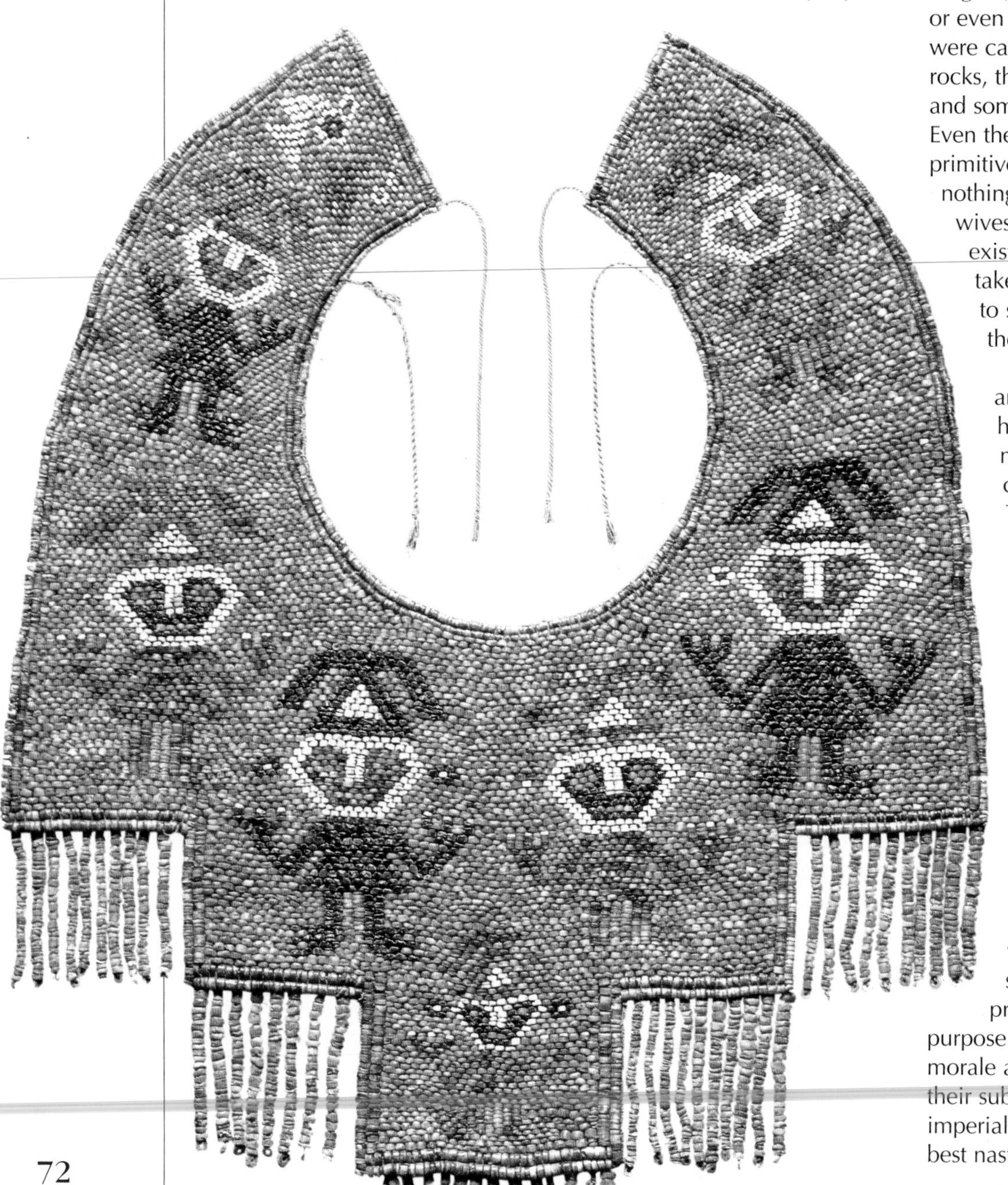

Over the past century, archaeological discoveries have shown that the old man's portrait was comprehensively wrong. The origins of agriculture predated the coming of the Inca by at least a couple of thousand years, and they were also preceded by a sequence of earlier civilizations, some of whose surviving artworks show a greater level of creative achievement than even Inca craftsmen attained. Yet tales of the savagery of preceding ages, which were easy to sustain with no written proof otherwise, served a purpose for rulers, boosting morale and helping persuade their subjects that life outside the imperial embrace would be at best nasty, brutish and short.

who did were impressed by the temple garden as much as by anything inside the building itself. The chronicler Pedro Cieza de Leon reported that in it "the earth consisted of lumps of fine gold, cunningly planted with blades of corn that were also made of gold – stalks, leaves and ears". Even the rakes and spades used to tend the living plants were made of precious metals, as were the pipes that brought water into the garden and the reservoirs where it was stored.

Originally the Coricancha contained images of the principal gods of all the major conquered provinces. The deities were there strictly on sufferance; insofar as the lands from which they came accepted Inca rule peacefully, the effigies were treated with all due honour, but at the first sign of rebellion, they were taken out into Cuzco's main square and publicly whipped to shame their followers back into obedience.

By the time of the Spanish conquest, however, the provincial deities had temples of their own in the capital, and the Coricancha's six chapels were given over to Inca deities. Besides Inti, these comprised the moon goddess Mama Kilya (see box, page 61), Illapa the thunder god, and the divinities representing the rainbow, the Pleiades and the planet Venus.

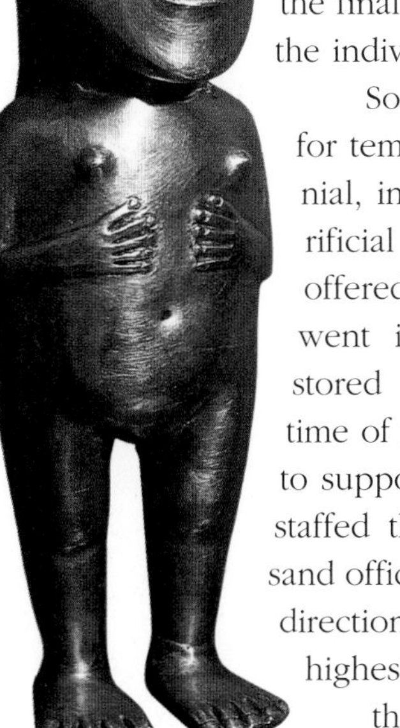

The "Virgins of the Sun" were girls of noble birth who were trained to perform religious rituals. This gold figurine dates from either the 13th or the 14th century.

Beyond Cuzco, another focal point of the Inti cult was Lake Titicaca, where Viracocha had first set the sun and moon in the sky. There was already an important temple on an island in the lake, and Pachacuti further endowed it after he gained control of the area in one of his military campaigns. On a second island nearby was a temple dedicated to the moon, and the priests and priestesses attending the two shrines visited each other on gaily decorated balsa rafts. Reportedly, the Titicaca temple was as richly endowed with gold as Coricancha itself, though its fittings disappeared without trace at the time of the conquest; local people later claimed that the priests had thrown them into the lake when they got word that the Spaniards were coming.

The enormous sums necessary to construct and support such establishments were collected through taxation. Subjects of the empire handed over a third of all their takings – paid in produce, for money was not used – for the welfare of the gods. A similar amount went to the emperor to support the imperial bureaucracy, leaving only the final third, the last to be garnered, for the individuals' personal use.

Some of the gods' share went to pay for temple construction and for ceremonial, including the vast numbers of sacrificial llamas and guinea-pigs that were offered up to them daily. Another share went into warehouses, where it was stored to provide emergency relief in time of famine. But the greater part went to support the small army of priests who staffed the larger temples. Several thousand officiated at the Coricancha under the direction of the Villac Umu, the empire's highest-ranked religious official. Usually the post was filled by one of the emperor's own brothers.

There were female priests, too, housed in the convent-like *acllahuasis* or "houses of the chosen women". The choosing was done at around the age of ten, when young girls distinguished by their high birth or beauty were selected for admission. As noviciates they were given instruction by older inmates known as *mamaconas*, literally "esteemed mothers", who taught them the skills of weaving, dyeing, conducting religious rites and preparing food and *chicha* beer. After three years they went to Cuzco to attend the Festival of the Sun, where the reigning Inca himself would pick some to serve as wives for himself, his fellow Inca nobles or for the provincial chiefs. The rest were married off ceremonially to Inti or to other gods.

They were expected to take vows to their celestial husbands seriously; those found guilty of taking earthly lovers were sentenced to be buried alive.

The Spaniards called these women Virgins of the Sun. As many as 4,000 served in the central *acllahuasi* in Cuzco, where their duties included the preparation of clothes for the Inca ruler – an onerous task, since he never wore the same garment twice. Others were dispatched to temples throughout the empire, where they prepared food for sacrifices, officiated at rituals or presided over shrines. Some were destined for a sadder fate, for female sacrificial victims were invariably selected from the chosen women's ranks.

Sacrifices to the Gods

Fortunately, the number of human sacrifices was limited, for although sacrifice was a daily occurrence throughout the empire, the victims were almost invariably llamas or guinea-pigs. The animals' blood would be offered up to the appropriate image of the god and then smeared over it. Other offerings deemed fit for the gods were food, coca leaves and textiles, which were either wrapped around the totem or burned in its presence. Small images of gold or silver might also be buried or hung by the shrine.

Public sacrifices were usually carried out in the open air, in fact most religious ceremonial was performed outside the temples, which were less places of worship than repositories for the images of the gods. In Cuzco a white llama was sacrificed to Inti daily, while a brown beast was offered up to Viracocha. At the start of each month, one hundred animals were dedicated to the gods in the presence of the Inca king himself.

The chief focuses for public worship, however, were the festivals which crowded the Inca year, providing vital psychological relief for a hard-working and tightly controlled populace. Under Pachacuti's reorganization, there were as many as 120 of these annually, giving life in the Inca lands its distinctive rhythm. Nearly all the feasts featured singing, dancing and open-air processions in which sacred images would be paraded through the streets – another parallel that the Spaniards noted with their own religion.

Major celebrations often stretched over several days. One such was Aymoray, marking the maize harvest in May, at which nobly born youths ceremonially circled Cuzco's main square with a gaily coloured rope, chanting hymns as they went. The Coya Raymi in September was a ceremony of purification featuring torchlight processions and river ablutions. The most important festival for the Incas themselves was Capac Raymi, at which future noblemen were initiated.

Yet for sheer spectacle none of the feast days can have rivalled the Inti Raymi, sacred to the sun god himself, which marked the start of work in the fields each June. The ceremonial highlight was a procession that left the Coricancha temple in Cuzco before sunrise. Only Inca noblemen could participate. Splendidly garbed in vicuna tunics and silk cloaks embroidered in silver and gold, they moved through the darkened streets carrying holy images that were protected from public gaze by elaborate feather canopies. Golden bracelets and anklets adorned their limbs, and discs of gold encircled their heads. When they reached the scene of the feast on a hillside outside the city, they lined up to await sunrise, forming a guard of honour for the reigning Inca, who sat a little apart on a low, golden throne.

As the solar disc edged its way above the horizon, the monarch rose to his feet and strode forward to intone a hymn to the sun. The other nobles took up the song, gradually increasing the volume as the flaming orb rose higher in the sky. Then the mood would lighten, and the men would spend the rest of the day chanting, dancing and drinking *chicha* beer, while llamas were sacrificed to Inti and girls dressed in long robes from the *acllahuasi* provided food on golden vessels. Only at twilight would the ceremonies come to a halt. Through the gathering darkness the participants would wend their way home, knowing they had paid fitting homage to Inti the life-giver, and so to the mythical forebear of their own Inca race.

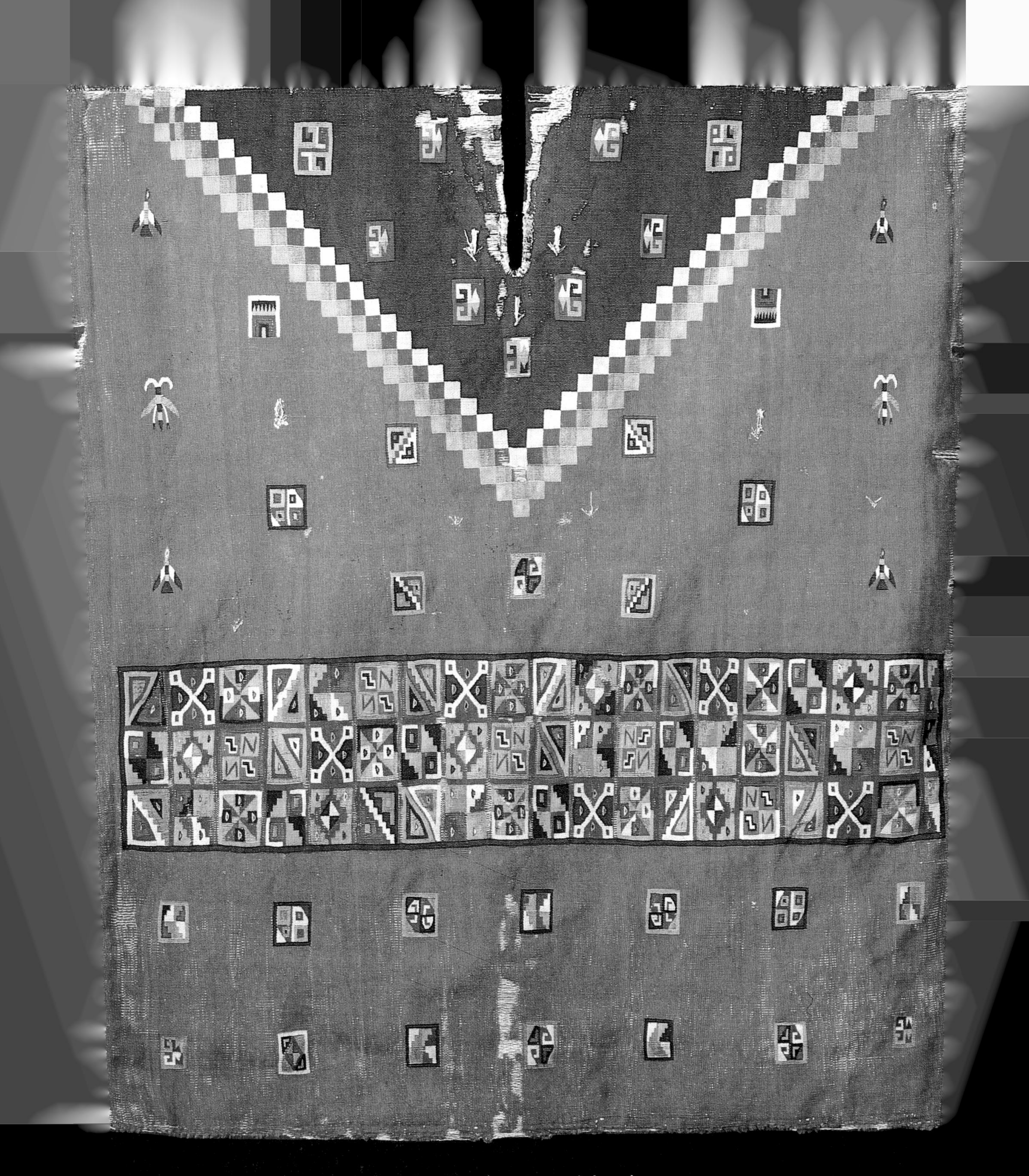

Special garments, such as this gorgeous Inca-period poncho, were worn during important festivals. This example's delicate weaving and complex

Nightfall at Noon

Barely one hundred years after Pachacuti started to build his empire, invaders from across the sea brought the entire Inca world crashing down. Traumatized, the survivors of the cataclysm struggled to come to terms with the disaster that had befallen them; as they themselves described it, night had fallen at noon.

Throughout its history, the Andean world had been familiar with disasters, but the Spanish conquest was different from anything that had gone before. There was nothing in the Indian world-view to prepare them for the shock, for to the people who had to confront them, Pizarro's men might almost have come from a different planet. Unlike the Indians, they wore beards and clothes that completely covered the body; they rode on the backs of terrifying animals; they communicated, apparently magically, by means of pieces of white cloth; and they controlled thunderbolts, directed with lethal effect from metal tubes.

Though the Inca troops soon found that these extraordinary beings were no more than mortal, the outcome of the confrontation was foreordained. There were two major factors in the defeat of the Incas. One was the technological gap that separated Inca slings, darts and quilted jackets from the metal armour and muskets of the Spaniards. The other was disease. The Europeans brought a host of illnesses, including smallpox, which devastated the Incas, wrecking morale.

Worse was to come than military defeat. The conquistadors showed a startling lack of respect for Inca customs. They invaded temples and palaces and took the virgins of the *acllahuasi* as concubines. Even the highest in the land were treated with contempt; when Manco Capac, the puppet Inca set up to serve Spanish interests, offended his new masters, they threw him into prison. There drunken soldiers urinated upon him as he lay in chains, while his jailer raped the Coya queen and boasted to him of the deed.

Fortunately the brutalities of the conquest were short-lived, and soon a new breed of Spaniards appeared who for the most part wanted to help the native peoples. Yet in their own way these churchmen increased the survivors' psychological disorientation. They taught that everything their charges had been brought up to believe was false. Shrines and temples were destroyed.

As their world collapsed, the Incas retreated into apathy and despair. Many simply lost the will to live. Most accepted the Catholic faith of the

An Inca warrior in his finery decorates the side of this wooden *kero* or drinking vessel. This object was made soon after the Spanish conquest and before the Inca empire was defeated.

conquerors more or less willingly, not least because in certain respects it bore some recognizable resemblance to their own traditional beliefs. Yet beneath the surface of Catholic orthodoxy, many traditional Andean ways survived more or less in secret. Diviners were still consulted and *huacas* were revered.

In time a form of normalcy returned, though with the native peoples now firmly at the bottom of the pile. The heirs of the Inca empire gradually came to terms with the foreign worldview that had been imposed on them, forming a hybrid culture that combined elements of both worlds. Yet the trauma of the conquest was not forgotten. And the event that came to symbolize it most keenly was the execution by the Spaniards of Atahualpa, the Inca who had so unwisely gone unarmed into Pizarro's camp that fateful day in 1532. A lament thought to date from the sixteenth century caught the cosmic significance of this event for the native peoples, who saw their link to Inti cruelly severed. It described the sun growing dark and the Earth refusing to swallow up the ruler's corpse, while mountains trembled and streams filled with tears.

The execution of Atahualpa recorded here by Poma de Ayala, c.AD1620, was a traumatic event for all Indians.

Even today the tragedy is regularly re-enacted in local festivals in the form of a play. Many versions of the drama have been recorded throughout Peru and in the Bolivian *altiplano*. In it, the Spaniards speak silently, moving their lips without utterance – a dramatic convention to indicate the incomprehensibility of their language. More mysteriously, they hand out 'leaves of maize' – writing paper – bearing messages no one can decipher. Faced with such impenetrable opponents, Atahualpa has no real hope; his execution becomes inevitable.

Return of the King

A legend that still circulates claims that the Inca, like such other great monarchs as King Arthur and Charlemagne, will one day return to right the wrongs of his people.

In the Inca version, Inkarrí – literally "Inca King" – was the divine son of the sun who at some unspecified time in the past, usually identified with the coming of the Spaniards, was foully tortured and beheaded. But, the stories claim, his head remains alive. It lies hidden to this day in a secret place while a new body slowly grows upon it. When the process is at last complete, Inkarrí will rise again to take his rightful place at the head of his people and to restore the glories of the lost civilization.

THE FORGOTTEN CITY

Hiram Bingham outside his tent at Machu Picchu.

Machu Picchu is probably South America's greatest archaeological site. But for centuries the fortified Inca city was hidden by thick vegetation, its whereabouts known only to a few local people. Only about eighty kilometres from Cuzco, Machu Picchu covered about thirteen square kilometres and was surrounded by terraced gardens. Its position between two peaks kept it secret from the Spaniards after the conquest and its existence was only discovered by the outside world in 1911 when Yale historian Hiram Bingham was guided to the ruins by a local boy. For some months, Bingham had been travelling through the Andes by mule, searching for the "lost city" in which the last Incas were believed to have lived.

Below: This stone, today known as "the Hitching Post of the Sun", stands in the open air. Its exact purpose is unknown but it may have been used for sacrifices or some other kind of ritual.

Above: Nearly 3000 steps connect the terraces that surround Machu Picchu. The city is still cut off from the rest of the Urubamba valley by dense undergrowth and rough terrain, making the approach today almost as mysterious and intriguing as it was in 1911.

Left: The shape of this window in the Temple of the Sun is typical of Inca architecture. Stones were hewn to fit together without the need for mortar. They were so carefully matched that during an earthquake they could move and then slip back into place.

Opposite: Machu Picchu lies at the end of the fertile Urubamba valley. It may have been settled by Inca colonizers, sent from the faraway capital of Cuzco to exploit the local ecology.

AFTER THE CONQUEST

When the Spaniards invaded South America, they expected to find a land filled with incalculable wealth, fabulous beasts, and the characters and creatures described in their own mythologies. The many wonders they actually encountered – the great civilizations, impenetrable jungles, mighty rivers and strange animals – only seemed to drive them to still wilder fantasies. Even as they were conquering the Inca empire, they were telling stories of a yet richer prize, the golden city of El Dorado, hidden further in the depths of the continent. In the reports and tales they brought home to Europe, they described the New World as a form of Utopia – a rediscovered Eden – but also as a place filled with demons and monsters. And as trade and travel increased, a new European mythology of South America began to develop.

At the same time, the beliefs of the Spanish and the Portuguese became a part of South America's own developing folklore. Today there are many native myths which share the conquistadors' view of South America as a deadly fairyland, luring travellers to their doom. Modern Andean folk tales tell of enchanted places such as the cone-shaped mountain of the Nustas, where on clear nights Inca princesses and the daughters of tribal chiefs can be seen dancing to the sound of otherworldly music. Anyone who is seduced by the spectacle is turned to stone.

The conquistadors appeared highly strange to the Incas. Dirty and ragged, they came with customs, tools and even animals that had never been seen before on South American soil. But because of the bitter civil war that then raged among the Incas, the invaders were mostly ignored. Soon, however, the conquistadors were entering native myth as demons, evil spirits and harbingers of apocalypse. In some cases these omens of doom became self-fulfilling prophecies. For example, in the sixteenth century the Guaraní peoples of Argentina, Brazil and Paraguay found colonial rule so oppressive that they were convinced the world was about to come to an end. They embarked on a series of desperate migrations across inhospitable country in pursuit of a mythical paradise, in the course of which their numbers were decimated, falling from 1.5 million in 1530 to 150,000 in just two hundred years. It is one of the tragic ironies of South American history that the myths clung to by native peoples to help them preserve their past and hold their culture together have also sometimes driven them to their own destruction.

Opposite: **A European explorer travels with a native escort in Jean-Baptiste Debret's lithograph, first published in 1834. The expedition was searching for the source of Lake Dos Patos in Brazil.**

Below: **This ornament, of the pre-Columbian era, is now in the famous Bogatá Gold Museum. Riches such as this inspired conquistadors to undertake perilous expeditions to mythical destinations.**

The Giants from the West

When the first Spaniards appeared on the coasts of the Inca empire, the locals did not know whether to fight them, fear them or worship them. The Incas believed in a confusing abundance of mythical beings who might one day arrive from the west, and the Spaniards could have proved to be any one of them.

The peoples of coastal Peru inherited ancient legends of invaders from the sea. Long ago, one of the legends said, newcomers arrived, some dressed in animal skins, some stark naked, in reed boats which were as large as ships. Nobody knew where these people came from, but to the tribes who lived along the coast they were truly monstrous. The head of an ordinary man would only come up to their knees and their eyes were the size of plates. They landed at Santa Elena, and made an encampment there whose ruins could still be seen by the early Spanish explorers. The area was practically a desert, but because of their great strength the giants were able to dig wells deep into solid rock until they found water which, because it came from so far down, was always sweet and cool. However, the native peoples of the coast grew to hate their new neighbours who had appetites fifty times as great as those of normal men. In an area where food was often scarce they took more than their share of fish from the sea and game from the forest, and they would also steal food whenever they got the chance, leaving their bitter neighbours hungry.

The giants were especially loathed because they forced both the local women and the local men to submit to them sexually, and because of their great size they always ended up crushing their unwilling partners. But the natives were powerless to do anything more than pray for divine vengeance and hope for a day when the dreadful giants would leave them in peace. Then one day a pillar of fire roared out of Heaven, revealing an angelic being with a sword of flame which consumed all of the giants, leaving nothing but a few of their skulls scattered on the ground.

Men from the Sea

Juan de Velasco, who wrote an early European history of Quito, speculated that the giants came to South America around the time of Christ. He also thought that other invaders arrived about six hundred years later. The Cara came in *balsas,* log ships which could carry up to fifty men. After populating the coast they soon moved into the mountains, and ruled Quito until the Inca took it from them in the fifteenth century. Yet another legendary invasion was led by the god-chief Naymlap who landed on the coast near Santa Elena. As soon as his followers came ashore, they built a temple and erected a green stone idol to honour him. After reigning for many years, Naymlap grew wings and flew off into the sky, leaving his empire to its fate.

When the conquistadors came on their horses they might well have resembled the towering western invaders of myth. Their skin, clothes and weapons were strange enough to the people of South America, but their appearance was rendered even more remarkable by the animals they rode. Horses were awesome creatures which nobody in South America had ever seen before. To the Incas, it was not immediately obvious that the newcomers were hostile. They could have been emissaries of Thunupa who many years before, having brought culture and law to South America, was said to have walked away into the west across the Pacific Ocean. In the north, the Europeans were referred to as *gagua,* after the supreme god and giver of light Chiminizagagua. However, as the list of their atrocities grew and the true nature of their mission became apparent, they were associated with the local devil, Suetiva, and their title was changed to *suegagua* – "demon with light".

The Patagonian Colossus

A popular belief in the gigantic stature of Patagonians survived in Europe for centuries after Antonio Pigafetta, who accompanied Magellan on the first voyage round the world, wrote a highly coloured account of his adventures. After rounding the Cape, Pigafetta's ship put into a cove to escape the winter weather. This gave Pigafetta a chance to add another story to his collection of tall tales.

According to Pigafetta's account, a naked giant appeared one day on the shore, dancing, singing and leaping in the air while pouring sand over his head. When a party from the ship approached him, the giant seemed astounded, and pointed upwards, thinking that they had come from Heaven. He was so enormous that the tallest of the sailors only came up to his waist. His huge face was painted red all over, except around his eyes where the skin was yellow. He had two hearts painted on his cheeks, and dyed white hair. When he was shown his own face in a steel mirror he was so terrified that he jumped back, knocking over four crewmen.

More giants arrived later. Two of the younger ones were put into chains, but their friends on the shore started firing arrows at the ship, killing one of the crew. Although the sailors had guns, they never hit a giant, because despite their bulk they never stood still, moving nimbly and running faster than horses.

Magellan's ship sailed past these mountains, the Carro Paine Grande, in Patagonia. For some of the Europeans, such sights gave substance to the myths they heard on their travels.

The Birth of the White People

The origin myths of many Amazon Basin tribes not only account for their own existence, but also describe the creation of their neighbours, explaining the many differences between them. So when white people began arriving – with their curious skin, guns, tools and insatiable greed – the tribal storytellers naturally made them a part of their mythology.

White people are often conceived as a result of some perverted act, or breaking of a taboo, which could be expected to bring evil into the world. A Shavante legend from the Xingu region of the Amazon Basin, tells how a boy called Tserebutuwe, a terrible glutton, kept sending his younger brother to beg for nuts from his mother. At first she gave him what he asked for, although the other villagers, and the boy's brother, were offended because he never saved any food, and would not share it with them. Eventually the mother lost her temper with Tserebutuwe and decided to teach him a lesson. She cut off a piece of her flesh, hid it among some nuts and then offered them to her unsuspecting son. He chewed on the flesh for a long time and swallowed a great deal of saliva before he realized what he had in his mouth. It made his belly swell up until he could hardly drag himself around, and he realized that his mother was taking her revenge on him by trying to turn him into a toad.

Tserebutuwe escaped into the forest, taking his mother's flesh with him so that he could fashion it into two wives to keep him company. When some boys from the village found him, he magically made their hair grow long, and after that many men came looking for him, asking for the same trick. Tserebutuwe became bored and frustrated with all the people visiting him, so he turned one of them into a toad to frighten them away. Then he turned his river home into ocean, and lived on the other side of it as a white man.

The Ayoreo of the northern Gran Chaco say that Corabe, the white butterfly, was once a girl with very pale skin. She was so beautiful that all the men wanted her, so she climbed a tall, slippery-barked tree and said that she would marry whoever could clamber up to join her. Nobody could manage the climb until, finally, the iguana reached the top. The pair were married, but all the other men were jealous and plotted to kill the iguana, so he and his wife had to run off and live far away from the Ayoreo, where they became the ancestors of all the white people.

White Tools of Treachery

In another myth, the whites and the Ayoreo once lived peacefully together until Angaye, chief of the whites, decided he was too important to touch the ground, and made the Ayoreo carry him everywhere. Tired of all this work, the Ayoreo fled to the Gran Chaco and settled there for good.

The Yupa say that white people's technology was invented to destroy them. It was made by a brilliant, evil girl who fled to Europe when the outraged Yupa killed her mother. But she said she would one day return with guns and armour. While adrift on the waves, she was impregnated by the ocean, and in Europe she gave birth to the first white men. These Europeans conquered South America specifically so that they could fulfil their ancestor's vow to punish the Yupa.

The Txukarramae tell of a girl who fell in love with a vast, red-headed caterpillar that she saw munching its way through the forest. They began courting and the girl soon became pregnant. But when her child was born it sucked her blood instead of her milk and she died. Her angry relatives burned the child and set fire to a nearby tree that was full of caterpillars. Some survived and were transformed into white people. They began to devour the forest, driving the locals from their lands.

Tales of a Merciless Paradise

Of all the stories brought back by the early Spanish explorers, none excited their European audiences more than accounts of flesh-eating savages and warrior women. Christopher Columbus claimed to have met cannibals on his first voyage, and heard accounts of an island populated only by women when he returned.

When the Spanish first encountered native legends about a race of rich, fierce, independent women, they naturally assumed that they had discovered the descendants of the Amazons – the female warriors of Greek myth. Initially, these women were thought to live on one of the Caribbean islands, which Columbus identified as Matenino, supposedly located near Hispaniola. Here they tolerated only occasional visits from men, and then for the sole purposes of breeding. But as more and more of the islands were explored, the legendary home of the Amazons retreated further and further into the jungles of the continent. Most people still thought that they would be found on an island, but now believed that it lay not in the sea, but in one of the great rivers of South America.

Francisco de Orellana was the first man to sail down the Amazon from the Andes to the sea, in 1541, and he claimed not only to have heard stories about the Amazons, but to have fought a battle with some of them. During a skirmish near an Indian village, the ship's priest, Fray Gaspar Carvajal, said that he could see ten or twelve women at the forefront of the native warriors, acting as if they were in command. It is not uncommon for South American native women to fight alongside the men, but Carvajal's Amazons could have stepped straight off a Classical Greek vase: they were extremely tall and robust, with fair skin and long hair twisted into plaits on top of their heads. Apparently they killed several of Orellana's crew with their bows and arrows. Later in the sixteenth century, Ulrich Schmidel, journeying north from Asunción, added yet more Grecian details to the South American Amazon legend. According to his accounts, the tribes he met told him stories about a country rich with gold and silver, which they all said was two month's journey from their own. This wealthy land was the home of the Amazons, who received visits from men only two or three times a year. If, as a result of these visits,

The Brazilian chief Camacan calls his people to battle in this 1834 lithograph by J.B. Debret. Fierce encounters with Amazonian warriors, both male and female, earned the jungle and its people a reputation at once noble and ruthlessly savage.

Flesh and Bone

As well as stories of fierce women, the European imagination delighted in tales of cannibalism which were both thrilling in their lurid depiction of savage practices, and politically expedient in their portrayal of a world of godless barbarism, which needed to be tamed by Christian missionaries.

Only a handful of peoples, including the Guayakí, Maué and Tapajo, practised both exocannibalism (eating flesh) and endocannibalism (consuming the ashes of bones). Most groups chose only one method, with endocannibalism usually found among the peoples of the upper Orinoco (such as the Waika and the Shiriana) and the western Amazon (such as the Tukano and the Conibo). It has been argued that eating flesh usually represented a fear of the dead body, and a wish to make it harmless by consuming it. Drinking the ashes of the bones, on the other hand, was a celebration of death as the fertilizing source of all life, and a way of sharing the dead body around the whole community. The Yanomami, for example, consider endocannibalism as the best possible way of expressing affection. The living can drink the ashes of the dead in a plantain brew, a drink which gives them the ability to see the spirits of their departed friends and relatives living in peace and tranquillity in the Yanomami Heaven called *hedu*.

This 16th-century engraving by Theodor De Bry is a highly imaginative portrayal of a cannibal feast inspired by tales from the jungle.

they gave birth to a boy, he was sent to live with his father. If the child was female, her right breast was burned to stop it growing, so she could use a bow and arrow more easily when she grew up.

The English explorer, Sir Walter Raleigh, claiming that he "had knowledge of all the rivers between Orinoque and Amazones", said that there were many Amazon nations in the Topago region. Every April, the kings of the neighbouring tribes would gather and the various Amazon queens would choose their mates. When they had taken their pick, their followers would draw lots to find partners from among the remaining tribal rulers. The men would stay with the Amazons for one month, feasting, dancing, drinking and making love, before being sent back to their own people. Raleigh denied that the Amazons cut off the breasts of their daughters, but agreed that they were bloodthirsty warriors who would kill any prisoners they took during battle.

The Brave Women

A Shavante myth from the upper reaches of the Xingu River, in Brazil, tells of a time when women were deadly fighters but chose not to live alone. Instead they fought as allies with the Shavante men, and helped them attack other tribes that dared to cross them.

Long ago, before there were any jaguars, the bravest men of the Shavante had all died while taking part in their regular raids to kill people who were not part of the tribe. So the women decided to take the place of these men, and went off to attack some white people. Although Europeans lived very far away in those days, distances were much shorter and it took the women only a few days to reach the houses that they thought belonged to the white people. But when they got there they found only spirits with flat, white faces, and bodies covered with feathers. The women were not sure if these were white people, because they had never seen any before. But they suspected they might be something more dangerous. Neither the spirits nor the women knew who should be more afraid, but finally the spirits ran off and the women looted their village. They took all the mats, baskets and weapons, just as they still do today in the Way'a Festival, which wards off evil. But on their way home they became ill with colds and boils. They all thought they were going to die, and were being punished because they had not planned the attack carefully as men do when they go into battle. However, by tending each other and singing songs to give themselves strength, they made it back to the Shavante village, where they were honoured by the men, and forgiven for their mistake in not planning the attack properly.

Despite routing the white men, the Shavante women were frightened by their opponents' ghastly pallor.

All the rivers of Brazil and Guyana have their own native legends about proud races of female warriors, with names such as the Husbandless Women, the Masterful Women, the Women-Living-Alone or even Great Lords. One story, found all along the banks and tributaries of the Amazon and Tocantins rivers, tells how all the single women of a village had gone to bathe on the banks of a river when they were approached by a big black cayman. He was very tame, and one by one they lay down and made love to him. The next day they went back to the same spot with meat and pies for their lover. The affair continued, until one day a fisherman saw what was going on and told the other men, who decided to ambush the cayman. They went to the river and hid, and one of them, disguising his voice, called to the beast. When the cayman emerged from the water, the men killed it and roasted its flesh for a celebratory feast. The next time the women came to the river, they could not understand why the cayman would not answer them, until one of them saw the remains of the men's meal and realized what had happened. To avenge their cayman lover they made clubs for themselves and began ambushing men and beating them to death. Gradually they wandered far from their original home, and formed a separate tribe, consisting only of women. They spurned the company of men and would only have sex with those who could beat them in a foot-race. They also killed all their male children.

In some myths, such as those of the Ramkokamekra of the Megrim River, a fierce foreign woman kidnaps boys to raise as her own, but then tries to eat them when they displease her. The Famished Old Woman – another name for the Pleiades – who tries to lure young boys into her cooking pot is a common character in Brazilian folklore. Although some explorers deny that there was ever much cannibalism in South America – and there was almost certainly less than the Spaniards claimed – it did once play a large part in the life and rituals of several native peoples, and still exists in some places. Often it was part of a complicated system of inter-tribal warfare and revenge, and myths may reflect the fact that the cannibal himself was often eaten in turn.

This macaw-feather headdress would have been worn by a man from the Rikbatska tribe. While myths may sometimes tell a different story, Indian men and women generally had separate social roles.

The Kayapó of Brazil say that the first lice used to crawl on an old man called Teeth-in-the-Head. He would get young girls to come and delouse him, but he had many sharp-toothed mouths hidden in his long hair, which would nip their fingers. Then, once he had acquired a taste of their blood, he would eat them. One girl ran away from him. She was helped by a heron that swallowed her whole, except for a single strand of hair which served to pull her out again after Teeth-in-the-Head had gone past. The cannibal found her again, though, and chased her to the side of a river, where she accidentally kicked a stick into the water. It was immediately attacked by piranha fish, which gave her an idea. She walked down to the water's edge, to make it look as if she had waded in, and then hid behind a tree. The cannibal, following her tracks, plunged headlong into the river, where he was eaten by piranhas. However, although he is no longer around to persecute women, his lice remain behind, feeding off people's scalps.

Tales of the Golden City

The legend of a lost city of gold, ruled by "men of metal", lured explorers and raiding expeditions to Peru from the early days of the conquest. Since then, there has scarcely been a country in South America that has not been claimed as the site of El Dorado.

When the Spaniards arrived on the west coast of South America, they heard stories from nearly all the peoples on the fringes of the Inca empire about a magical kingdom where the roads and buildings were made of gold. It was ruled by a powerful priest-king, called El Dorado, "the Gilded One", because even his body was covered in gold. These legends were probably native hearsay about the great cities of the Inca, but even after the Spaniards had conquered and pillaged the empire, they refused to accept that they had found the fabled kingdom, and continued to search for it in the mountains and jungles beyond Peru.

As it happened, the tales had some foundation in fact. In pre-Chibcha times, the "Gilded One" was the new ruler of the region around Lake Guatavita in the Colombian mountains behind Santa Fe de Bogotá, who would make an offering of gold to the god of the lake to mark his accession to the throne. Before the ceremony, the ruler-to-be spent some time fasting in a cave, before marching to the lakeside where priests stripped him of his royal robes and covered his body in a layer of fine gold dust. The newly-gilded king then sailed out into the middle of the lake to make his offering, accompanied by four local chieftains who were also dusted with powdered gold. In the centre of the lake, the new ruler dived into the water, washing off all the gold so the gods could take it. Gradually, El Dorado lost its original meaning, and instead of referring to a person came to be haphazardly applied to any mythical golden city.

"People of Metal"

The Guaraní, from the basin of the Plate River, told tales of a golden city that almost certainly derived from fifteenth-century raiding expeditions across the Chaco. They captured piles of gold and silver from peaceful tribes that were subjects of the Incas, and returned with stories about "people of metal" living to the north.

From these excursions, the idea of a golden land called Paititi spread throughout Paraguay. It was combined with existing myths. Eventually it came to be said that Paititi lay in a magic lake

Right: **The discovery of jewellery such as this gold Tairona pendant, AD900–1550, led some conquistadors to believe that El Dorado was in Colombia.**

Left: **Tales of the legendary king, El Dorado, stimulated the imaginations of Western chroniclers. This 16th-century engraving shows him being painted with gold.**

The Golden Condor

The* Derrotero de Valverde (Account of Valverde) *contains detailed instructions on how to find a great Inca treasure in the mountains of Ecuador. But although exact copies of the original document still exist, nobody has ever been able to find the gold.

In 1584 the young soldier Juan Valverde fell in love with a native girl and together they ran away to her home village, Pillaro, high in the Andean mountains. There they lived until a Spanish patrol arrived three years later. Valverde was terrified that he would be caught and executed as a deserter, and decided that he and his wife should return to Spain. To help pay for the journey, the village elders told him that the Inca general Ruminahui had hidden a store of gold in the mountains.

After three weeks, Valverde returned with treasures that included a golden condor, with emerald eyes and outstretched silver wings. But the village headman declared that the condor had to remain hidden until the Europeans had been driven from the Andes and the Inca empire re-established. The bird was returned, but even without it Valverde now had enough gold to make him rich.

When the half-illiterate conquistador returned to Spain laden with dozens of crudely formed gold bars, King Charles V ordered him to reveal the source of his wealth, or have it confiscated. The *Account of Valverde* reveals that the great golden condor lies, with many other idols, in an artificial lake in the Llanganuti mountains. The route to it – through forests, along rivers and over daisy-covered hills – is described in detail, starting from the village of Pillaro. King Charles sent several expeditions in search of the lake, all of which were defeated by weather, starvation and exhaustion. In the nineteenth century, the Spanish botanist Antonio Guzman found some ancient Inca mines in the area, but could not locate the treasure. In this century, even helicopter reconnaissance has proved useless in the face of fog, high altitude and bad weather.

called Cuni-Cuni, which was the source of the Paraguay River and was guarded by a jaguar-lizard called Teyu-Yagua. According to the tale, all of the population wore gold and silver ornaments. In 1526, Sebastian Cabot sailed the Parana and Paraguay rivers to find them.

Other expeditions soon followed. In 1530, a German knight called Ambros von Alfinger set off inland from the Venezuelan coast. Instead of finding the legendary city, the knight became legendary himself – for his cruelty. His provisions were carried by native slaves, chained together by neck-rings. When these slaves became exhausted, von Alfinger beheaded them to save the trouble of unfastening the links. Eventually, the knight was killed by a native arrow.

Incredible cruelty, followed by the violent death of the oppressor became a feature of El Dorado expeditions. When Francisco de Orellana arrived at the Coca River in 1541, on the journey that would eventually lead him to sail down the Amazon, his intention was to join Gonzalo Pizarro (brother of the conqueror) on a quest to find El Dorado. He had set out from Quito three weeks after Pizarro, but had no trouble following his trail, because it was signposted with corpses. Pizarro left Quito with 400 Spanish soldiers, 4000 native slaves, 2000 dogs, 4000 pigs for food, and a herd of llamas. He returned a year later with eighty starving men, a sorry testament to his doomed search for Lake Guatavita.

A Legend of Lost Souls

The El Dorado of the Omaguas was thought to be in the upper reaches of the Orinoco River, near the mythical Lake Parima, said to lie on the Venezuelan-Guyanan border. Diego de Ortaz set out to find it in 1537. Decades later one of his men, called Juan Martínez, stumbled from the jungle, starved and exhausted, and swore with his dying breath that he had met the Gilded One. There is still a popular Chilean myth about the City of Caesars, which has solid gold streets and lies somewhere in the south of the country on the borders of a mountain lake. The city is named after an expedition to find it, sponsored by Sebastian Cabot and led by Francisco César. Not only are its exact whereabouts unknown, it is also invisible, and seems to contain elements of native ideas about the afterlife. The people who live there do not have to work, and they live for ever. Anyone who happens upon the City of Caesars by chance, however, forgets all about it, including the route back, once they leave. This enchanted city will only appear at the end of the world.

The ceremony at Lake Guatavita, depicted in this finely-made pre-Columbian Chibcha gold *tunjo*, or raft, is believed to have been the source of all the tales about a mythic golden city somewhere in the South American hinterland. Beautiful gold objects such as this continued to inspire treasure hunters for centuries after the conquest.

To this day stories are told of travellers lost in the jungle in search of the golden city. Many of them are probably apocryphal. The most famous disappearance of the twentieth century was that of the British Colonel Fawcett, his son and a companion. In the 1920s, they went looking for a lost city of gold in the Mato Grosso, deep in the rainforest. Fawcett was an experienced surveyor and explorer. They never returned, although for several years sightings were reported.

The Legend of Thunupa

Christian missionaries, who wanted to believe that the word of Christ had already reached South America, seized on *altiplano* legends of a great, bearded, cross-bearing teacher who, so legends say, came wandering into their lives from the distant north.

The Spaniards who explored the regions around Tiahuanaco encountered many stories about a hero or demigod called Thunupa who came to Peru in ancient times with five disciples. According to legend, Thunupa was tall and dignified, with blue eyes and a beard. He wore a sleeveless shirt that reached to his knees, and carried a large wooden cross on his back.

Further north, there are similar legends about a bearded old man called Nemptequeteve who came from the east to teach people how to grow fruit and vegetables, weave cotton and build houses. One of the customs he left behind him was the practice of putting crosses at the graves of snake-bite victims. Thunupa's first journey in South America was said to have been to the city of Carapacu, where he criticized the chief, Makuri, for being a cruel warmonger. Finally the local priests drove Makuri from the city.

There are numerous local legends about Thunupa's travels through the Andes. In villages above Lake Titicaca, the people used to say that he banished demons to the mountains. Before Thunupa came, they said, the demons had forced them to make human sacrifices. Out of gratitude, the villagers built him a home near Jauja, close to the spot where Thunupa had seen a female demon and a village man making love and had turned them both to stone.

Despite his wisdom, Thunupa earned himself many enemies. He was puritanical, and violently opposed to drink or promiscuity. When he preached in the town of Sicasica, the people burned his house down. After this, Thunupa returned to Carapacu, where one of his disciples had converted the daughter of chief Makuri. Thunupa baptized the girl, which enraged her father so much that he had Thunupa and his

The sun sets behind the Kalasasaya Gateway, at Tiahuanaco, Bolivia, built AD400–800. The temple, at its most majestic during equinox, reflects the ancient belief in the primacy of the sun as an object of worship. Early Christian missionaries struggled against this elemental view of religion when spreading their own teachings. Finding Christian parallels with local beliefs, therefore, played an important role in helping the new imagery supplant such enduring visions of god.

disciples beaten to death. Thunupa's body was placed in a reed boat, and pushed out on to Lake Titicaca. The boat sped away from the bank, astonishing the onlookers. It crashed into the shore at Cochamarca so powerfully that it created the source of the Desaquadero River, whose waters carried the body away to sea.

A Christian Apostle

The Augustinian Fathers claimed Thunupa as one of the Apostles. Some thought he was Saint Thomas, and emphasized his kindness and his martyrdom. Others thought he was Saint Bartholomew, and focused on the miracles with which he punished the guilty. According to an early seventeenth-century story, Thunupa's killers tried to burn his cross. When that failed, along with their attempts to cut it to pieces and sink it in the lake, they decided to bury it underground, where it remained until it was discovered by the Augustinians in 1569.

According to some historians, Thunupa still survives in modern Andean culture in the figure of Ekeko, a god of good fortune who is celebrated at the Alasitas – fairs held annually in La Paz, Cochabamba and Oruro. Tiny figures of the god, often dressed in a red poncho and peaked cap, are worn as amulets, and miniature houses, trucks and even money are sold on the market stalls. People will buy these objects and make an offering to Ekeko, hoping to acquire the real thing.

The First Christians

The Craho and the Ramkokamekra, among other Gé-speaking peoples of Brazil, believe that Christians were created by the culture hero Awkee, whom they came to identify with Dom Pedro II, Emperor of Brazil from 1831 to 1889.

Awkee, who some say was fathered by the sun and some by a rattlesnake, became a white man and a Christian after his uncles tried to burn him to death. He built a huge brick house for himself, with pots, woven cloths and other merchandise inside, guarded by a soldier at the door. When his oldest uncle passed by, Awkee called him in, telling him not to be afraid. He then told him that he had saved all the others from turning white by living apart from them. Awkee loaded up his uncle with gifts, and sent him back to the village to ask others to come and visit. The uncle showed off his new trousers, his knife and his glass beads, and the next morning all the people gathered and went off to visit Awkee. He gave them a cow and flour to feast on, and that night they all slept on the floor outside his house.

In the morning, Awkee called to the young boys and girls and invited them to choose what they wanted from his possessions. As soon as they came inside he barred the door and told his soldier to fire shots into the air to frighten all the older people away. Then he turned all the boys and girls into whites, and hit them over the head so that they forgot their parents and where they came from, and in this way they became Christians.

Dom Pedro de Alcántara, Emperor of Brazil (1831–1889).

Spirits of the Mountains

Pachamama is the ancient Andean goddess whose body is the Earth. Despite the efforts of the missionaries, she survived the Spanish conquest, and along with other old mountain gods – called *apus* – is often worshipped on Christian holy days.

The Peruvians of the Ocongate say that once God had made the world he gave it to Pachamama and the *apus* to develop as they wished and then retired to a distant place. Pachamama, who called herself "Saint Earth", had the task of creating and nurturing the land that God had made. She is the mother of everything, absorbing her children back into her body when they die, and according to herbalists it is her blood that flows through plants and gives them their healing powers. Pachamama decreed that the people of the Andes should burn coca leaves and spread them over the Earth to please her, and that they should make sacrifices to her, especially on the feast days of Saint James, The Immaculate Conception and Our Lady of the Purification, at Christmas and New Year and on the Thursday before Ash Wednesday. On these occasions, Pachamama is offered anything from beer to plants to guinea-pigs, and people frequently sacrifice sheep and llamas to her as well. At one time the sacrifices included human life.

Whenever the Incas found a potato or an ear of maize with a peculiar shape, they made offerings to it as though it were a representative of Pachamama. They believed that she was usually asleep, but that during the period of Jujay, from July to August, her body opened up to receive new seed, as well as sacrifices and public adulation. During Jujay the Earth was not only alive, it was also ravenous or even angry, and liable to release evil powers into the world. At this time of year people would be careful not to incur her wrath.

Despite her fierce reputation, Pachamama is often compared to the Virgin Mary. In the mining communities of Peru and Bolivia, she is the gentle Virgin of the Mineshaft, who protects the workers from the devilish owner of the mines, known as "Uncle", and his demonic female companion. This view of mine-owners, and the beneficial influence of Pachamama, is reflected in a legend from the

Pachamama, mother spirit of the Earth to whom all human life returns on death, proved an enduring goddess. With the advent of Christianity, her worship was allied with that of the Virgin Mary, ensuring that in timeless places such as here, where the Illiniza volcano towers over an exposed mountain valley in Ecuador, the ancient spirits of the Andes lived on.

early days of colonialism. The Spaniards running one particular silver mine worked their native labourers to the point of collapse. The workers tried fighting back, but all their protests were mercilessly quelled. In desperation the workers prayed to the mountain for help and either the spirit of the mountain, or Pachamama herself, took pity on them and came to their aid. One night a native mule-handler, on his way to the mineshaft, met a man he had never seen before who told him the road was blocked and urged him to turn back. But the handler was curious, so he returned later and hid by the track. After a short while there appeared an endless line of mules, each carrying a load of silver slowly past him and away from the mine. Suddenly one of the animals collapsed and broke its leg. The handler rushed up and unpacked it, burying the silver by the roadside so he could fetch it later. But when he returned, the silver and the mule were gone. Where the mule had been lying was a beetle with a broken leg. The merciful spirit in the mountain had turned all the local beetles into mules to carry away every bit of ore in the mines, so that the Spaniards no longer had any reason to stay in the area, and would leave the natives in peace.

Just as the Incas absorbed much of the imagery of the cultures they conquered, so Christianity was influenced by local belief. This 18th-century painting shows the Virgin Mary in Cerro Rico, the rich hill of Potosí, Bolivia, echoing the ancient belief that the landscape was home to Pachamama.

A Cult of Santa Maria

The popularity of the Virgin Mary owes as much to the essentially feudal system imposed by the Spanish government after the conquest as to the spiritual orientation of native Indians.

The Virgin Mary was a popular figure for many of the early Spanish settlers. Mixing easily with the maternal cult of Pachamama, her image soon became widespread among the native Indians as well. As the Immaculate Protectress she was the natural refuge from the manifold tragedies of disease, death and social exclusion that came with the invasion.

In the Christian faith, Mary is subordinate to her son. As such she won the sympathies of a class kept in place by a rigid spiritual hierarchy. Native Indians and *mestizos* were banned from the priesthood by the First Council of Mexico in 1555 and, three years later, from reading the scriptures altogether. This prohibition was not lifted until the end of the eighteenth century and the publication of the first vernacular translation of the Bible in 1790.

Damned Souls and Flying Heads

The mountains and jungles of South America have always been said to crawl with parasitic spirits, that survive by feeding on the vitality of the living. Such creatures are still believed to exist in Christianized South America, where they are thought of as souls of the damned.

The Andean mountains are, allegedly, home to legions of condemned spirits, called *condenados*. These are souls that have been refused entry to Heaven because of some mortal sin, such as incest or murder, and are doomed to spend eternity trying to climb to paradise up the steep, slippery sides of the mountain glaciers, always slipping back before they reach the top. To sustain themselves in their task they feed on humans, sucking out their life-force after tricking their victims into making love. Another type of vampire is the *ñaqaq*, which takes the form of a man who mesmerizes his victims before draining off their body fat. Once home, the victim will wither and die.

Other such fiends include some of the strangest beings in modern Andean folklore, the *cabezas voladoras*, or flying heads. These creatures are witches, who spend most of the time living normal lives as mortal women. This folk tale is typical. A young man began a relationship with a girl in his village. Although she was very affectionate, she told him that he should never call at her home on Tuesdays or Fridays. At first he thought nothing of this, but as the months went by he began to wonder why he couldn't visit her, not realizing that on those days she detached her head and sent it swooping through the streets, looking for people to eat. The young man became more and more impatient with his girlfriend's secrecy, until one Tuesday he decided to call on her. There was no answer when he knocked on the door, so he put his eye to one of the knots in the wood and peered inside, where he saw his girlfriend's headless body lying on the bed, screeching through its neck. He realized at once that he was involved with a witch, and summoning all his courage he went inside and smeared ashes on the stump of her neck. When the flying head returned, the ashes stopped it reattaching itself to the body, and the man, who had hidden beneath the bed to see what

A sight such as this pre-Inca cemetery on the coast near Lima would not necessarily have shocked those from local cultures who believed that the life-force of humans did not die with their bodies. But for anyone travelling in the mountains, an encounter with a *condenado,* a spirit condemned to wander through the harsh, desolate valleys of the Andes, could be terrifying indeed.

Shape Shifters

***Condenados**, spirits condemned to roam the Earth for eternity after committing a mortal sin, fooled human beings by changing shape and voice to imitate anyone they pleased. They could be male, but it was the females who were the most feared.*

One particular story about a *condenado* is often retold. One evening, not too long ago, a young man was travelling alone along a lonely mountain road. He was surprised to come across a beautiful woman – and even more so when she threw herself at him, offering him her body for the night. The young man succumbed to her blandishments without hestation and the couple made love until dawn. But as the sun rose in the sky, the woman told the young man that she was a *condenado.* Then she disappeared and within weeks the young man had wasted away and died.

Sometimes *condenados* were cannibals rather than seducers. In one fable, a young mother waiting for the return of her husband saw a woman in a white jacket hurrying along at dusk. The woman looked cold so the mother invited her in to keep her company for the night. Once they were inside, the housewife asked the woman in white to hold her two-year-old baby while she knelt down to light the fire. But when she rose to her feet again and turned round, she saw that the woman's mouth was covered with blood and that her baby had been eaten down to the waist. The housewife herself only escaped by hiding among a herd of cows, whose panicked lowing frightened the *condenado.*

The smiling face of the spirit on this Chancay textile, AD1100–1476, from coastal Peru, belies its true nature, suggested by the dragon headdress and the two figures in its belly.

happened, could not stop himself from laughing. Immediately the head fastened itself to his shoulder and, when he could not force it off, he ran screaming into the countryside and carried on running until he came to some prickly pears. When he had calmed down, he asked the head if it was hungry. It said it was, so he offered to fetch some pears from the nearby tree. He laid his poncho on the ground so the head could wait for him while he picked them, but as soon as the teeth released their grip on his shoulder he sprinted off. The head waited for another victim and soon fastened itself to a passing deer, which bolted through the prickly pears. The witch's hair tangled in their spines and she was killed.

Spirits commonly appear as disembodied heads among the native peoples of South America. The gourd rattle, which is one of the most important of the shaman's tools, is often decorated to resemble such a head. A Warao shaman, for example, attaches feathers, which he refers to as "hair", to his rattle and cuts mouths into it so that its powerful spirit voice can speak out loud and help him control other supernatural entities. The modern folklore about evil flying heads may be a reminder of the Church's early attempts to vilify shamanism. The witches probably make their deadly transformations on Tuesdays and Fridays because these were regarded as evil days in the medieval Christian calendar.

Myth as History

In the eyes of the colonized peoples of South America, white men were often demons or monsters. The history of the conquest itself is also articulated in various types of myth, and many of the continent's revolutionary movements have been led by people claiming to be traditional culture heroes reborn, or servants of the old gods.

Among native Andeans the time of the Incas is thought of as a golden age. The era we live in now is one of decay and sacrilege. Memories of the conquest that brought about this decline are preserved in Peru in a play called *The Tragedy and Death of Atahualpa*, which is performed in villages and towns on or around Christian feast days. The play follows Atahualpa, the last reigning Inca, from the prophetic nightmares that first warn him of the arrival of bearded foreigners to his execution at the hands of Pizarro. But some legends go further, claiming that Atahualpa's severed head, buried by the Spaniards, continues to live, and is slowly sprouting a new body. As the present age draws to a close, Atahualpa will burst from the earth as Inkarri (a name that combines the word Inca with *rey*, the Spanish word for king). He will drive the Europeans from South America, re-establishing the Inca empire, and the order of the cosmos.

Some Andeans, however, have not been prepared to wait passively for the end of time. Followers of the Taqui Ongo (Dance of the Pleiades) movement which swept through Peru in the 1560s not only foretold the apocalypse, but tried to make it happen by allowing the *huacas*, or local gods, to possess their bodies. When they danced, they claimed, the old deities would be reborn and would overthrow the Christian god. Colonial authorities were quick to stamp out the uprising, imprisoning and exiling the leaders.

This late-17th-century, oil-on-cotton picture of an archangel with a gun, from the Lake Titicaca school, shows how Christian iconography became mixed with more traditional imagery. Christian angels were imagined as armed Spanish grandees.

For the Pajonal Campa, white men are the new form taken by demons that have escaped from their confinement. But they also believe that the universe goes through cycles of cosmic destruction in order to renew itself, and that, just as shamans defeated the demons in the past, so spiritual heroes will arise who can do the same again. Inspired by this conviction, the Campa undertook a series of rebellions in the eighteenth century. One of the most successful rebel leaders was Juan Santos, who in 1742 declared that he was Apu Inca, the legitimate heir of Atahualpa. Advocating the strict observation of Campa rituals among his followers, Juan Santos acquired an army of followers and destroyed twenty-seven Franciscan missions. Over the next ten years, the the old Campa, Amuesha and Piro territories were restored to native rule. Mystery still surrounds the death of Juan Santos, and according to the Campa he is immortal. His tomb is on the Cerro de la Sal, and for more than 150 years devotees laid a tunic on his grave annually, in the hope that he would return to wear it.

Juan Santos wished to become emperor of Peru, and set up his own church, with priests ordained from Rome. Such was the influence of Christianity on many of the native messianic legends, evident even when they are being used to fight Christianity. The Makiritare, for example, claim that their creator being Wanadi, who will return at the end of the world, was crucified on the orders of the cruel Fadre – a word which derived from *padre*, or priest.

This chapel in the jungle in the Guayana highlands, Venezuela, was built by Spanish Capuchin monks in 1724.

Messianic Migrations

Mass pilgrimages to a paradisiacal land were a common theme in tribal folklore before the conquest, but became more important afterwards, as a way of fleeing a world tainted by the Europeans.

In one of their tales of the end of the world, the Guaraní of Argentina, Brazil and Paraguay tell how everybody becomes so weighed down by their faults that their souls cannot fly to the magic lands where they can be renewed. This fate is more likely since the Spanish conquest, for the Europeans brought food and behaviour that were not created by the gods. A second tale says that shamans will one day lighten all bodies and souls and lead the people to The Land Without Evil, a paradise across the sea, where everyone will become immortal.

The first recorded mass migration in pursuit of this land was in 1515. In the next few decades whole populations, convinced that the end of the world was at hand, set off on exhausting journeys across the continent. Entire tribes were exterminated on these treks, by war, disease and fatigue. The Apapocuva, led by the shaman-prophet Nimbiarapony, followed the Tiete River to the eastern coast, but turned back to the centre of the continent when they hit the Atlantic. Only two people survived, but the shaman amassed a fresh following in the Mato Grosso, and set off on a new search for the centre of the universe. He died in 1905.

TREASURES FOR THE AFTERLIFE

One of South America's most compelling enigmas surrounds ancient practices of burial and ritual sacrifice. Tombs, often placed at *huacas*, or holy places, sometimes dug deep into the highest mountain peaks, suggest both mystery and terror: for the bodies found within them included not only princes and kings who had passed away, but, in some cases, people, even children, sacrificed for the greater good of their society. Such burials furnished a nobleman with the materials to live on in death as he had in life. By appeasing ancestors, they might also ensure a reign of peace for a new ruler, or a bountiful harvest for the nation. In addition, elaborate burials forged a spiritual bond between communities and the landscape and, in the case of the interment of the great Inca, offered a focus for disparate peoples spread out across the vast and distant plains.

Right: **Gold and silver ornaments accompany the Old Lord of Sipan in the grave. The gold-and-turquoise warrior with owl headdress in the centre recalls his prowess in battle. Such examples of ancestor worship were as much for the benefit of the living as for the dead.**

Above: **The remains of these two adobe pyramids in the Lambayeque valley, northern Peru, mark an important Moche burial site. From AD100 to AD300, several generations of the Lords of Sipan were buried here amid an array of gold and turquoise objects which testified to a wealth they would keep beyond death.**

Right: **This wooden mask, with shell eyes, bound with a tapestry band, would have given human form to a mummified individual of status who, curled into a foetal position, would have been put in a crevice or other such natural grave. This Inca example dates from c.14th century.**

Above: Figurines, such as this female form, *c.*1500, are common to Inca burial sites. Fascinated with an ideal other world, the Inca often rendered it in miniature; hence the sacrifice of children, who as small adults, were symbols of innocence and perfection.

Left: This wooden hand grasps a disc of the sun. It was found in a Chimu burial mound, dating from *c.*AD900–1500, and is probably less a religious symbol than a potent political one. Chimu rulers sought power and influence through conquest rather than industry. Overrunning areas that had flourished under the Moche, like the Lambayeque valley *(far left)*, they let irrigation canals fall into ruin while taking on local craftsmen to produce goods which offered prestige and political influence. The symbolism of the piece would have fitted a politically accomplished king.

THE FOREST PEOPLE

An Amazonian chief once informed a group of early colonial explorers that the tribes of the rainforest were more numerous than grains of sand. And with forest peoples spread out beyond the lush Amazonian jungles to areas as varied as the thickly wooded savannah of Gran Chaco, around the Paraguay River, or the semi-desert scrub of northern Venezuela, his extravagant claim is given some perspective. For each tribe has its own dialect, sometimes its own language and, invariably, its own mythology.

Despite all the differences between the stories, however, the legends of the forest peoples share a common frame of reference and serve a unified purpose. By describing a world filled with the spirits of animals, plants, trees and humans, the myths reflect the astonishing richness of life in the rainforest. Physically, the area contains eighty percent of the world's 1.5 million known living organisms. And, for the indigenous cultures, the area is as diverse in spirits, each of which is capable of transforming into another.

Such a fluid, potentially dangerous world has to be controlled. Most tribes have a shaman who attempts to exert some influence over the supernatural world. By using chants, trances or hallucinogenic plants, the shaman fights battles or strikes deals with the spirits, negotiating for a specific purpose: the curing of the sick, the success of the hunt, or the calming of a storm. In general, however, it is myths that articulate the careful balance between the physical and spiritual worlds, attesting to the power of language to impose order on a chaotic universe. These tales of an age when jaguars possessed fire, people were prey to strange beasts and animals could talk, serve to make sense of the origins of the superabundant rainforest. They are also cautionary, warning of the possibility of the return of disorder.

Many of the rituals practised by the forest peoples use masks, music and dancing to recreate the magic, and the confusion, of the mythological age. These rituals are important because, in the native imagination, many of the elements that make up an ordered world, be they male or female, animal or mineral, are naturally dangerous, even hostile, to each other. From time to time the boundaries between them must be broken down so that the world can be refreshed, and then put back together, recreated, just as if they were being made for the first time.

Above: **The raw beauty of the forest is reflected in the jewellery made by its inhabitants, such as this pendant from Mato Grosso made from animal claws and cotton.**

Opposite: **The rainforest has kept its secrets for longer than any other place on Earth except the ocean depths. Even today, some tribes rarely see visitors from the outside world.**

The Making of Mankind

Each society has its own account of the origins of human life. The Lengua say that people were made by a giant beetle, the Mbyá that the first humans hatched from eggs. But one particular theme stalks most of these tales: that life sprang from the dark necessity of death.

The Desana tell how the first of their tribe was swallowed at birth by the Mother of Snakes who kept him in her belly as she slept within the depths of a river. Only when the dreadful snake was killed, cut open and the child released, could humankind develop. For the Makiritare of Venezuela, however, the being whose sacrifice enabled life to flourish was a man-eating jaguar. The hero twins, Iureke and Shikiemona, persuaded Manuwa, the jaguar spirit, to swing on the giant vine that connected Heaven and Earth at that time. They knew that the jaguar's insatiable appetite had given him a chronic flatulence that would propel him further and further into the air. On one enormous swing, the twins rushed up into the sky and cut the vine, sending Manuwa reeling through space to the edge of the world, where he fell, breaking his bones and condemned to an obscurity from which he is yet to return.

Sometimes, however, life is made possible by the death of the first people themselves. The

With most of the drama of the rainforest taking place high above them in the canopy, the forest tribes saw in the treetops the eternal struggles of spirits exemplified by the story of Manuwa the jaguar who swung to his fate on a giant forest vine.

Caraja say that the earliest beings lived in the Underworld. Because nobody fell sick or died there, it soon became overcrowded. So the people climbed up to the surface of the Earth to escape the congestion, but in doing so, they suffered a tragic fate – they became mortal.

The notion that mankind came from the Earth is taken up by the Guayakí of Paraguay. One of their origin myths describes their ancestors scratching their way to the Earth's surface using their nails. They became human when they learned to stand on two legs by dragging themselves upright against a wall.

Many tales tell how mankind is not only from the Earth, but of the earth, fashioned from dust and clay. According to the Makiritare, their supreme spirit, Wanadi, made the first man by taking clay from Mount Dekuhana. After shaping it and firing it, he lit a cigar and blew smoke on the figure, bringing it to life. The new man, Wahnatu, was the grandfather of all

Sounds Made Flesh

For many groups, sounds are the physical manifestation of spirits, their utterance essentially linked with creation itself. Ritual songs and noises, therefore, assume a great significance and the art of naming becomes a powerful and sacred act.

For most native peoples, the naming of an individual is one of the most important events in a lifetime. Many hold that one's body is merely the physical representation of one's name. Naming is thus often a task for a shaman, who will fly into the spirit world to find the appropriate syllables. Similarly, people from the Waiwai tribe on the Mapuera River hold their infants up to the moon which will name the child itself.

Chants are also held to be the physical manifestation of spirits. The Karina from Venezuela believe that there are sounds, called *wara,* which are the true forms of all animals. A *wara* can take on a bodily form, in which it can be hunted, but the rest of the time it only exists as a noise in human language. Many creation myths throughout South America echo the idea that creatures can be called into existence simply by uttering their names.

The Baniwa hero, Kuai, was said to be the first person to have passages in his body which allowed him to eat, breathe and defecate, making him the first being to experience the cycle of birth, life and death. He emerged when the supreme being, Yaperikuli, made a water serpent pregnant using only the power of his thought. Many years later Yaperikuli sent a cosmic fire that destroyed Kuai, and as he died, sounds emerged from his bodily passages. A mooing, tooting sound blew from his anus as a paxiuba tree grew there. The *waliadoa*, or "little sister song", dripped from his eyes when they produced tears. There was, in fact, a sound for everything that poured from Kuai's body. And because the Baniwa believe that Kuai was the child of the supreme being's knowledge, these songs and sounds are their way of understanding the whole of creation.

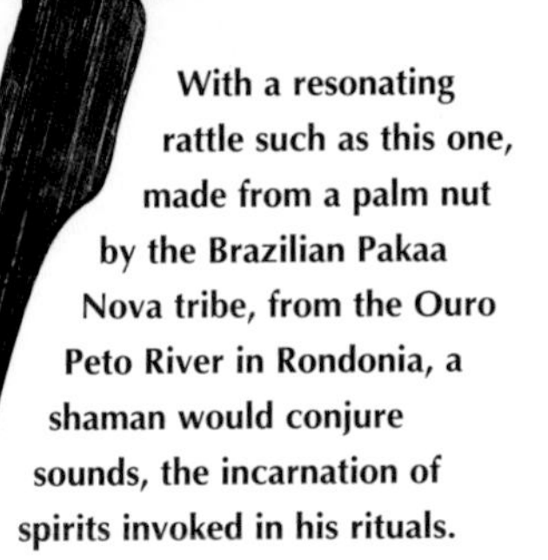

With a resonating rattle such as this one, made from a palm nut by the Brazilian Pakaa Nova tribe, from the Ouro Peto River in Rondonia, a shaman would conjure sounds, the incarnation of spirits invoked in his rituals.

How Outsiders Were Made

Even the most isolated groups have some contact with outsiders, and although a tribe's main concern is with its own origins, many myths explain how other races came into being.

Foreigners are usually described as late-comers. According to the Bororo, their own ancestor was the survivor of a great flood, whereas the first whites, blacks and other forest peoples were created much later, by a bored monkey banging a stick into the ground. The Yanomami of Brazil and Venezuela say that there was once a terrible fight in one of their villages near the headwaters of a river. A certain adolescent, who was supposed to be secluded in a sacred hut, joined in, and because the seclusion taboo was broken, the river flooded and washed all the brawlers downstream, where they were eaten by giant otters and black caymans. Their blood formed a froth on the river surface, and a supernatural being called Remori gathered this into his cupped hands and spoke to it, creating foreigners and giving them their languages. This is why the Yanomami describe the tongues of others as "ghostlike". Unusually, the Chamacoco of Paraguay say that the supreme being made all the other races first, and by the time he came to make them he was in such a hurry he made them flawed, which is why the Chamacoco consider themselves stupid and slow to learn.

the Makiritare. But he could only be created after all the original beings – the first birds, the sky people, Huiio the great snake and mistress of the waters – had drunk themselves into a state of ecstasy and left the Earth for Lake Akuena in the centre of Heaven. In this tale, the Earth was purged further by a great flood, caused when a cosmic tree was cut down to make the first garden. Wahnatu was created to tend the first cultivated plants.

As people of the forest, however, many of these tribes see their origins in vegetation, rather than the earth. When Makonaima stripped bark from a silk-cotton tree and threw it into the air, the pieces that caught the wind became birds, the pieces that landed on the water became fish, and those that landed on the ground became animals or humans of the Carib race, who gave their name to the Caribbean. In one of their origin myths, the Chamacoco of Paraguay say they came from a giant tree, that was chopped down by a hunter who heard singing and laughter coming from it. The whole Chamacoco people, young and old, marched cheerily out of the fallen trunk.

The pattern on this clay storage jar for *chicha,* a kind of beer, evokes the shell of a water turtle, an animal familiar to the Canelos Quichua, who lived on Ecuador's Bobonaza River.

The Roots of Social Difference

Origin myths often explain more than the existence of people and can even offer explanations of details such as social order as well. The Guajiro tell how their hero Mareiwa was born under an olive tree not far from present-day Nazareth, in Colombia. His mother was an old woman and his father may have been a god. He created a woman for himself, called Borunka, who became the mother of all the Guajiro. To feed his children, Mareiwa sent all the birds to far-off lands to eat the fruits of the plants there, and when they came back they spread the seeds in their droppings. He then gave each man a pair of domestic animals, either goats, donkeys, cows, horses or pigs, and dispersed the Guajiro into their many clans, which still exist today, each identifying with its own totemic animal.

Originally the totemic animals were to be human, but they offended Mareiwa by eating the livestock that he had given to the Guajiro. Mareiwa punished them by leaving them in their primitive state and making each of them a symbol of the people that they had robbed. So, because the king of the turkey buzzards ate a cow belonging to the Epiayait, the turkey buzzard became the totemic animal of that clan and, in the same way, the Uriana tribe were given the jaguar as their totemic animal and the Ipuana, the hawk.

The Guajiro provide a good example of how the myths of a single tribe may contradict each other. In one story, the clans were named by the wise hermit Utta, after a monkey had tried to give them titles that were obscene. But in a different version the obscenities were the brainchild of Utta himself, in the form of a woodpecker.

An alternative Guajiro origin myth says that the first beings were birds. One day Mareiwa told them to build houses while he was away. When he returned and saw that they had only built nests, he was disgusted and decided that he needed to make some more intelligent creatures. So he took some clay and moulded it into dolls. While he was working, he ordered the cucarachero bird to sing to the figures, telling them what colour they were and which clay they were made of. When he had finished, he asked the grandfather of the woodpecker to name them and assign them clans. Finally, all the dolls came to life.

Heaven and Earth

South American Indians imagine a universe with many layers. The Waiwai say there are five: the Earth, the Underworld and three separate heavens. The Yukuna of Brazil have seven heavens, and in every layer lives a particular kind of people.

The Earth and sky were not always quite so far apart. The Chamacoco even say that their positions were reversed until, one day, the sky could take no more of being trampled underfoot by people and animals. So it begged the Earth to swap and eventually the Earth agreed. In a number of myths, the Earth and sky had to be separated to impose order on the universe, so life could evolve. According to the Wayapi of Guyana, the world was originally nothing but a dark place of larvae, mildew and mushrooms. The Earth and sky were set in place by two teams of architects, one in each realm. But at first they did not lift the sky high enough, so the heavenly team dressed themselves in the tail feathers of the red macaw and other brightly coloured birds, and danced until the sky soared up to where it is now. Then they made all the stars to provide light for the world, while the earthly architects erected four giant posts at the edges of everything to hold the sky firmly in place. The Wayapi believe that during a lunar eclipse the world is in danger of reverting to its original state of chaos and a careful watch is kept for any signs that they might be turning into mushrooms.

The task of separating the layers of the cosmos is sometimes fulfilled by a central world tree with its roots in one realm and its crown in another. This tree is a giant pindo palm for the

Spectacular caps such as this Karajan one from Mato Grosso, Brazil, were worn during ceremonies initiating boys to adulthood. Its mosaic of scarlet macaw feathers evokes the gods who dressed as birds to separate Earth and sky.

Guaraní, a moriche for the Warao, a silk-cotton tree for the Shipibo and a paxiuba palm for the Baniwa and many others. The Chamacoco world tree, a prickly pear, used to hold the Earth and sky close together, and men would climb it to get honey, which it provided in abundance. One story tells of some fatherless children who never got any honey and were beaten by other, healthier children. Their angry mother decided to teach everyone a lesson. She turned herself into an insect and began to eat away at the tree, until it crashed to the Earth. Suddenly released by the tree, the sky shot off to where it is now, with all but three or four of the men marooned in it. They were turned into the stars, sun and moon.

Some supernatural beings migrated to the heavens voluntarily. The Tupari of the Mato Grosso region of Brazil say that once there were

Traffic Between the Worlds

Even when the layers of the universe have been separated from each other, and the world tree or connecting vines have been cut down, it is still sometimes possible to travel between them.

The Canelos Quichua of Ecuador believe that weather beings act as intermediaries between the Earth and sky. Fog transports life upward, while rain brings spirits and other celestial creatures down to the Earth. Birds are also messengers, carrying songs between Heaven, Earth and the Underworld. Along with other South American peoples, they also think that the giant anaconda, that lives in the rivers, can connect the watery regions with the sky by turning itself into a rainbow.

For the Canelos Quichua, even ordinary people can travel between the two worlds. Husbands and wives sometimes make dream voyages together, and wake hours before dawn to compare and interpret their experiences. In most cultures, however, the realms have to be linked by a shaman, who usually journeys between them while in a trance induced by some hallucinogenic drug. The Waiwai shaman, for example, drinks *kaahi*, which he prepares from a vine said to originate on the banks of Lake Akuena in the centre of Heaven. He is then able to send his soul to the layer of Heaven that holds his spirit helpers, or to the mountain where the Father of Peccaries lives, or to the swampy Underworld of the anaconda people. Once there he can negotiate with the spirit world on behalf of his terrestrial people. He may have been sent to rescue the kidnapped souls of the sick, or to bargain for a rich supply of animals to be sent to Earth for his people to hunt.

***Topus*, like this figure made by the Tapirape tribe, were messengers of thunder that attacked young shamans.**

Bringers of Change

Not all societies concern themselves with creation myths, or creator gods. The Waiwai, for example, claim to know nothing about the beginning of things, because the world has always existed, and their people have always lived in it.

Supreme beings who made the universe from nothing are comparatively rare in South American myths. In the myths of many cultures, the idea of a creator is replaced by legends about a great transformer.

In the origin tales of the Campa, from the forests of eastern Peru, the transformer Avireri appeared with his grandson in a world that already existed, but seemed to be filled with little other than Campas. So Avireri turned the Campa people into whatever they most resembled. Every time Avireri's grandson pointed at some people and asked what they looked like, Avireri would answer him and then change them accordingly.

A creator may also make the world by naming it or, more often, by dreaming it. The Witoto of Colombia say that in the beginning there was no reality, just a mysterious illusion. Nainvema, "he who possesses what is not present", used his breath to draw this mirage into his dreams, which he then fashioned into a thread so he could bind it. Exploring the illusion to its depths, he found it was completely empty, so he stamped on its base and made the solid earth.

Some supreme beings are halfway between creators and transformers. The Baniwa tell how the supernatural jaguar Yaperikuli made the Earth by playing a trumpet over a pebble produced by his son, Kuai. The pebble opened like a balloon and grew with each note of the trumpet. Although Yaperikuli created Kuai solely with the power of thought, his own origins are mysterious and hazily described by the Baniwa. It seems that even before Yaperikuli there was a forest of man-beasts that killed and ate indiscriminately. A bone from one of their victims was retrieved from a river by a grandmother and placed in a gourd, where it produced the three crickets that were Yaperikuli's first manifestation. Everything that he created was an act of vengeance against the primordial beings who had destroyed his ancestor.

The jaguar on the top of this Waura bowl and the fish markings below symbolize two key aspects of the universe: the power of land and sea.

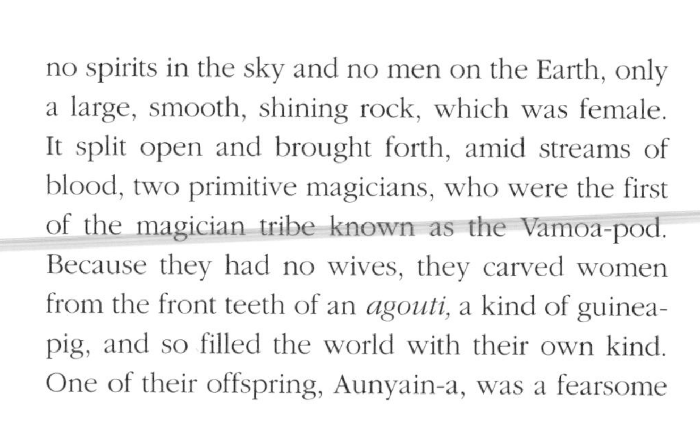

no spirits in the sky and no men on the Earth, only a large, smooth, shining rock, which was female. It split open and brought forth, amid streams of blood, two primitive magicians, who were the first of the magician tribe known as the Vamoa-pod. Because they had no wives, they carved women from the front teeth of an *agouti,* a kind of guinea-pig, and so filled the world with their own kind. One of their offspring, Aunyain-a, was a fearsome beast with tusks like a boar who had a taste for his neighbours' children. Everyone was so afraid of him that when one day he went out hunting the rest of the Vamoa-pod decided to escape by climbing a tall creeper to Heaven.

When Aunyain-a found everyone had gone he tried to follow them up the vine, but a parrot bit through it and the monster crashed to Earth. His body broke into pieces, with his arms and legs changing into iguanas and caymans and his fingers and toes turning into all the smaller lizards. Vultures ate his head and torso, and since then the primitive magicians have lived in the sky as spirit beings. They are invisible to ordinary people, and can only be seen by shamans.

Some cultures, on the other hand, say that human life originated in the sky. The Warao of the Orinoco were once sky people until one day a hunter searching for a lost arrow saw a hole at his feet. Down below there was a world filled with pigs, deer and other game, so he made himself a rope and went down to have a look. When he returned days later he was so full of stories of the abundant new world he had discovered, that all the other Warao decided to follow him down. The young men went first, then the elders, then the children and finally the wives. However, the last wife was too fat to squeeze through the hole. She became stuck, and nobody could free her, so the opening back into the sky became blocked for ever. The Matado of Gran Chaco state that men have always lived on the Earth as beasts. One day, they say, a group of women came from the sky on a long cord to steal their food. When a bird chewed through the cord, though, the women ended up having to marry the men and found the human race.

A Warao hunter chases birds high among the clouds unaware of the animal world of lizards, toads and caymans that flourishes far beneath him. The idea that human life actually started in the sky, rather than emerging from the Earth, is a common one among the tribes of the Amazon jungle.

Sun, Moon and Stars

Although some native peoples say that the sun created the universe, they mean an invisible sun that now lives in a Heaven beyond human sight. The sun and moon that we can see today are inferior spirit beings that, according to most storytellers, used to live on Earth.

All native stories about the sun and moon attempt to explain why they divide the sky between them. A folk tale from Brazil says that the sun and moon wanted to marry, but discovered that their union would destroy the world because the sun would grow too hot and burn, and the moon would weep too much and drown it. So they separated, and now never meet at all.

The eastern Toba, who believe that the sun is a woman, say that she was once attacked by a short black man called Napalpi, who tried to block her path. She could only escape him by fleeing to the west and taking a secret underground path across the Underworld sky before re-emerging in the east, a desperate journey that she continues to make to this day. The moon, Awoik, is a man who lives in the north and amuses himself by constantly changing his shape, from pot-bellied and ugly to handsome and athletic and back again.

Among the smaller societies the sun and moon are usually both male, and either brothers or friends. The moon is always smaller, slower or more stupid, which is why the sun has the sky during daytime, and the moon is left in darkness. The Bororo of the Mato Grosso explain the waxing and

The Toba believe that the sun is a woman. At sunset she escapes into the Underworld from the man who pursues her.

Fearsome Skies at Night

The movements of the constellations provide a calendar that allows the natives of South America to mark off the seasons. As a result, the birth of the stars is widely thought of as the birth of time itself – a terrible event, which destroyed the first beings and brought mortality into the world.

The Toba of the eastern Chaco have origin myths for more than thirty heavenly bodies, and all of them are stories of a devastating fire, a universal deluge or the first ever hunt. The whole of the dark Coalsack nebula is the head of a rhea, a small flightless bird, whose body is the constellation Ophiuchus, and whose leg is the part of the Milky Way extending down from Scorpius. The rhea was chased into the sky by a boy and his dog, who turned into two of the Centauri stars. Other versions of the story say that the two Centauri stars were dogs, the ancestors of all today's hounds, that were made from the breasts of two old women.

Some constellations are widely described as game or water animals, because their appearance, or indeed their absence, in the sky is a sign that life is about to be renewed at the end of the dry season. The Karina say that the tapir, a small pig-like creature that searches for sustenance by night, is the master of food, because at one time only he knew the whereabouts of the all-providing allepantepo tree. When he was destroyed by the divine twins Pia and Makunaima, he entered the sky as the Hyades, while his killers joined him in the stars as Orion and the Pleiades.

According to some stories, the constellations were created during a cosmic hunt. These Ribaktsa tribal spears, from Mato Grosso, were also used in spiritual combat by shamans.

waning of the moon with various stories about the twins Meri and Ari. One day, while out hunting, they came upon some jaguars that chased them through the forest. Meri, the sun, was faster and more nimble and was able to reach a tall, hard-barked angelim tree. As he climbed, he greased the trunk behind him, so that the jaguars could not follow. Ari, the moon, had to take refuge in a nearby genipap tree. Although he greased the trunk like his brother, the tree was so short, and its bark so soft, that the jaguars easily climbed up and ate him. But Meri quickly gathered Ari's remains and smeared them on an effigy he had made out of sticks and a termite nest. He then spread medicinal herbs over the figure and left it overnight. When he returned in the morning, the termite nest had grown to become the head of his brother, and the pieces of wood had turned into his limbs and trunk. But there was still no sign of life. So Meri crouched down by one of Ari's ears and, gathering his strength, yelled that hideous beasts were chasing after him. And, terrified by the voice of the sun, Ari forgot that he was dead and leapt to his feet, whole again.

Deluge and Regeneration

The cosmic flood is one of the most important events in South American mythology. It almost always destroys the old world, leaving only a few survivors to repopulate the Earth and make it as we know it today.

Great floods are often associated with serpents. The first of several cataclysmic Waiwai floods was caused, according to one of their myths, when a teenage girl was wandering by a river. She was seen by anacondas living there who fell in love with her and in their passion whipped up such a great storm that the girl's grandmother hid her in a clay pot. The Apinaye also say their deluge was caused by a serpent. In their flood myth, the great shapeless snake Kangeroti made his way inland from the ocean to make the Tocantins and Araguaia rivers, bringing with him the tumultuous waters of the deep.

This wooden scraper from the Kamayura tribe is carved in the shape of a wading bird. The egg of such a bird was said to contain the sea.

The Makiritare of the Orinoco valley link the flood to the death and dismemberment of a water snake. They believe that the creator took the invisible sounds that would one day turn into all the world's creatures and hid them in a stone egg until the time was right for them to hatch. Nuna, the hungry moon, stole the egg, but his sister Frimene sneaked it back and hid it inside her. During the night Nuna crept in to his sister and tried to take back the egg by force. The only way Frimene could escape was to turn herself into the rainbow-serpent, Huiio, mistress of the waters. But this meant that the seeds of all Earth's creatures were now trapped in an egg which was itself trapped inside the body of a serpent. In order to free it, a group of hunters waited for Huiio to appear in the sky as a rainbow. When at last they saw her stretched out across the sky, the men let fly a volley of arrows into her. The egg fell from the sky and landed on a river rock, smashing it open and releasing its contents. But the hunters were so excited by what they had done that when the body of Huiio crashed to the Earth they rushed forward and grabbed it, cutting it up to eat the flesh and bathing in the river of her blood. The fluids, though, poured ceaselessly from her body, and engulfed the whole of the Earth. Thus the act of creation was followed by a process of destruction, a typical feature of much South American myth.

The Revenge of Kuamachi

A single tribe may have many stories about previous ages. The Makiritare have an alternative flood legend, which begins when Wlaha, the Pleiades, and some of his friends killed Kuamachi's mother, the evening star. To get his revenge, Kuamachi lured Wlaha and the others up into a tall dewaka tree, by telling them how ripe its fruits were. When they were high in the branches, Kuamachi picked a luscious fruit and dropped it to the ground, where it smashed, releasing water that flooded the forest. He then made a canoe so he could escape from the tree, and once he was afloat he created all the deadly animals of the water: piranhas, anacondas, stingrays and caymans. Then, with a bow and arrow, he began to shoot the followers of Wlaha from the branches of the dewaka tree. One by one they fell into the water and were eaten by Kuamachi's animals, until the river ran red with their blood. Wlaha, who was still in the tree, called down to the gored and half-dead survivors, and together they climbed into Heaven on a ladder of arrows, where they cower to this day.

Dark Waters of Retribution

The story of Kuamachi combines two common themes: the idea of a flood arising from a tree or its fruits, and the belief that it was caused as an act of vengeance. Retribution, however, need not be for anything as serious as murder. A flood is often the punishment for transgressions as seemingly minor as curiosity, as in the Guajiro story of the first man, who became intrigued by a pelican's egg. He would spend his time pestering the mother to tell him what was in her egg but she would always reply that it was a secret that only she could know. Then one day he discovered it unguarded and, seizing his chance, he broke into it. But as soon as he had cracked the shell, the sea poured forth uncontrollably, flooding the surrounding area. The man only managed to stem the flow of water by throwing rocks at it.

The punishing flood, however, need not always be an engulfing flow of water. The Kayapó of Brazil say that once they lived in a state of unbroken daylight, because night was kept safe in a gourd. The people wanted some darkness, though, in order to get some sleep. So they went to the keeper of the gourd and begged him for the secret of night and he eventually passed the gourd over, telling them that they must wait until they got back to their village before opening it. But the impatient Kayapó peeked into the jar before they got home, and the night spilled all over the Earth. The Kayapó, who missed their chance to become the masters of the night, now blame themselves for the darkness that descends at the end of each and every day, which to them is poisonous and stinging, penetrating everywhere.

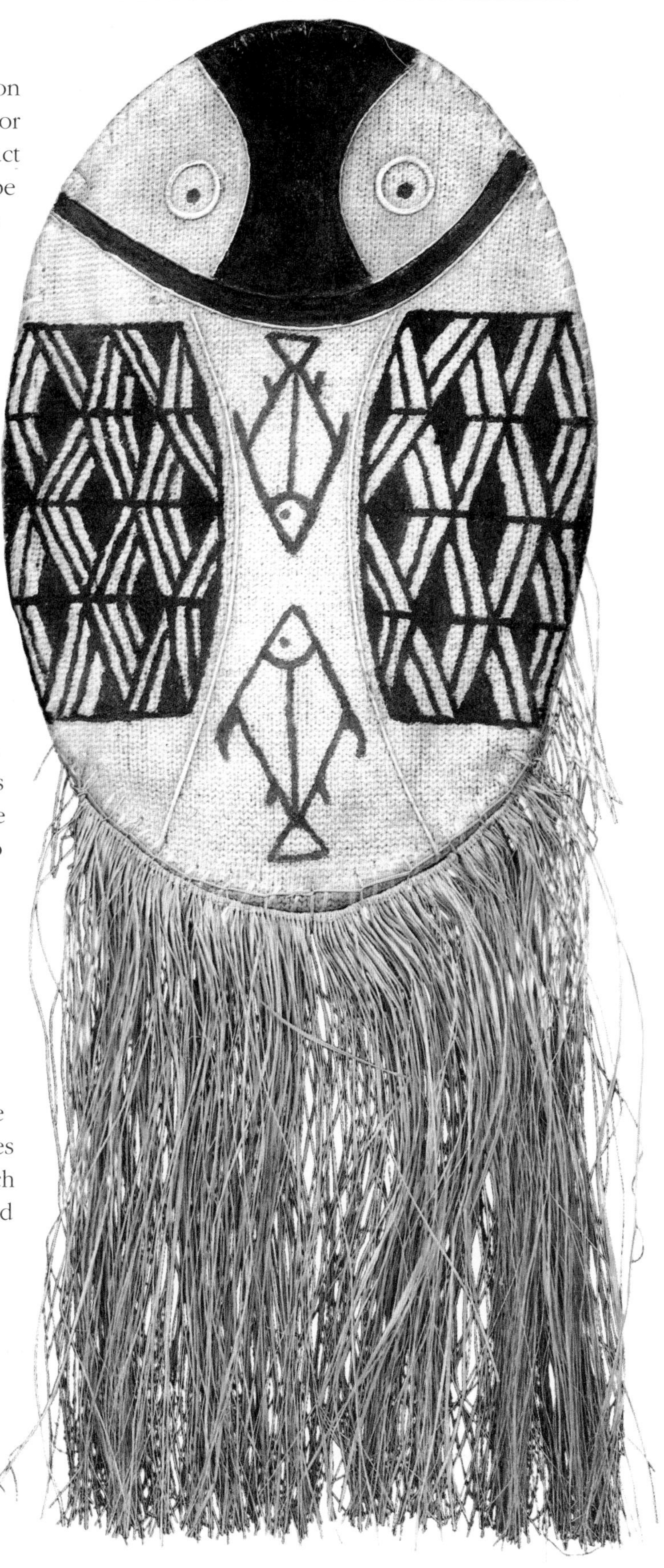

During harvest and fishing ceremonies a shaman wore this mask. Made from fibres and mineral pigments, coloured black with dye from the genipap tree, it is from the Kamayura tribe who dwelt by Lake Ipavu, in Mato Grosso, Brazil. For these people the deluge marked not so much a moment of disaster as the coming of the ocean, and with it the bounty that became their livelihood.

The Tree of Life

The forest peoples know that their own welfare depends on the trees which give them fruit, game and shelter. Some of their legends contain a wealth of practical information about the plants and animals around them, while others, more revered, recall a perfect time when food was plentiful and did not need to be farmed or hunted.

The peoples of the Paraguay River, near the Brazilian border, value the rare yobec mapic liana, which they say was provided by the creator spirit as a great, universal source of food. A malicious imp heard about the plant, though, and decided to spoil it by spilling a pitcher of tears over it, which shrivelled its flesh and ruined the taste by making it too salty. When the creator saw what had happened, he consoled the people, and showed them how to use the liana to season their food. They learned how to burn the plant and use its ashes as salt, a skill they still practise today.

Early European explorers noted that the Ackawoi, who live near the Orinoco, became very solemn when they told the story of their creator, Makonaima, and his miraculous tree. In the beginning of the world, Makonaima created all the birds and animals, gave them the power of speech, and placed his son Sigu to rule over them. Makonaima then made them a single tree which bore all the edible fruits of the Earth. This tree, though, was first discovered by a small rodent, the *agouti*, who decided to keep its existence a secret. The other animals noticed that the *agouti* grew fat and sleek-coated, but had no idea why. So Sigu sent the woodpecker to spy on him. But the bird's constant tapping gave him away and the *agouti* was careful not to lead him to the tree. So next Sigu sent the rat, whose stealth and cunning allowed him to discover the secret.

When Sigu was told, he decided to chop down the tree and spread its fruits throughout the Earth. He organized all the animals into teams to help him, but the monkey kept distracting everyone else, so Sigu sent him off to fetch water, with only a sieve to carry it in. When he cut through the tree trunk, Sigu discovered that the stump was full of water and stocked full of fish. But the water began to rise so quickly that Sigu had to cover the trunk with a basket. The vengeful monkey, however, took it away and the Earth was flooded.

Thinking quickly, Sigu sealed up the animals that could not climb in a cave, and took the others with him into a tall cocorite tree, where they all spent a sleepless night, dropping cocorite seeds from time to time and listening for a splash to see if the floods had subsided. When day came, the waters had gone, but now all the rivers were filled

Aspects of the story of Sigu are played out each rainy season when the Varzea area of rainforest floods. Tubular roots allow this tree to survive the sudden change to an aquatic ecosystem.

How Manioc Came into the World

Stories often tell how manioc was first brought to the world by a supernatural being. Through the foolishness of men, however, the provider is sacrificed, forcing people to learn the secrets of the crop themselves and cultivate a true respect for the food that has fed them for centuries.

The Jivaro believe that manioc was introduced to the world by a short, fat woman called Nunghui who possessed supernatural powers. Despite her strangeness, she was well respected because her son could make manioc simply by uttering its name. One day Nunghui asked some of the village women to look after her son, but while he was in their care a group of children, jealous of the talent that made him so special to the village, broke into the hut where he was staying and threw ash in his eyes, killing him instantly. The people, who did not know how to grow manioc, became desperate. As punishment for letting her son out of her care, Nunghui was forced to live underground.

But ever since, Nunghui has pushed the manioc up from under the soil, and dances with the roots to make them grow. Gardeners still perform rites to attract Nunghui to their plots of land to ensure a fruitful crop. Other peoples, especially in the northwest Amazon, say that manioc grew from the corpse of a white child born to a virgin, or from a maiden who asked to be buried alive.

with fish from the magic tree trunk. The creatures Sigu had protected descended to repopulate the Earth, but all were changed by their experience, either in appearance or behaviour.

Some, such as the *arauta*, which is a kind of monkey, stayed in the trees, howling in memory of their cold, uncomfortable night sheltering from the floods. The cayman – which many forest peoples believe to be tongueless – had eaten some animals in all the confusion. When he was accused of this, however, he denied eating anything at all, so his tongue was ripped out in punishment for lying. The trumpeter bird, seeing insects and larvae struggling in the morning mud, became hungry and plunged down to gorge himself. But he was attacked by the ants, that ate away his legs until they became the emaciated stalks that they are today. According to the story, the seeds of the miraculous tree are now so widely dispersed that gathering food has become a difficult task for all the animals and humans as well.

Men and Women

Many societies divide the whole universe, all objects, work, activities and rituals, into male and female, with powerful taboos preventing men and women from doing any task ascribed to the other sex. These customs are justified by myths of an ancient conflict between the sexes, before they co-operated to create human life as it is today.

In common with many other forest peoples, the Desana of the upper Amazon have different origin myths for men and women. They tell how the earliest male beings descended on a snake-canoe from a uterus in the sky, where they were conceived by the rays of the sun. The first female was the daughter of the acaru fish who, attracted from the water by the light of fires by which men danced and feasted, made love to a Desana man.

Such trouble-free encounters between the sexes, however, are rare in South American mythology. The Toba believe that once only males lived on the Earth. Every day when they came back from hunting, they discovered that the food stored away from the previous day had vanished. One day the parrot stayed behind to keep watch, and saw a group of women descend from the sky on a cord. They came to steal the food, and when they saw the parrot guarding it they pressed up close to him and pretended to argue over who should have him as a husband. Some say it is possible to tell the age of a parrot by looking at its tongue, so one of the women asked him to open his mouth so she could see how young he was. When he did as she requested she thrust a burning coal inside, singeing his tongue so that he could not call for help. The women then escaped with the food, and the parrot, which has a black tongue to this day, was too embarrassed to tell anyone what had happened to him.

These clay effigies from the Karaja tribe on the Araguaia River in Mato Grosso, Brazil, were made as dolls by mothers for their children. The bodies of both figures are painted with red dye from urucu seeds and with blue-black dye extracted from the

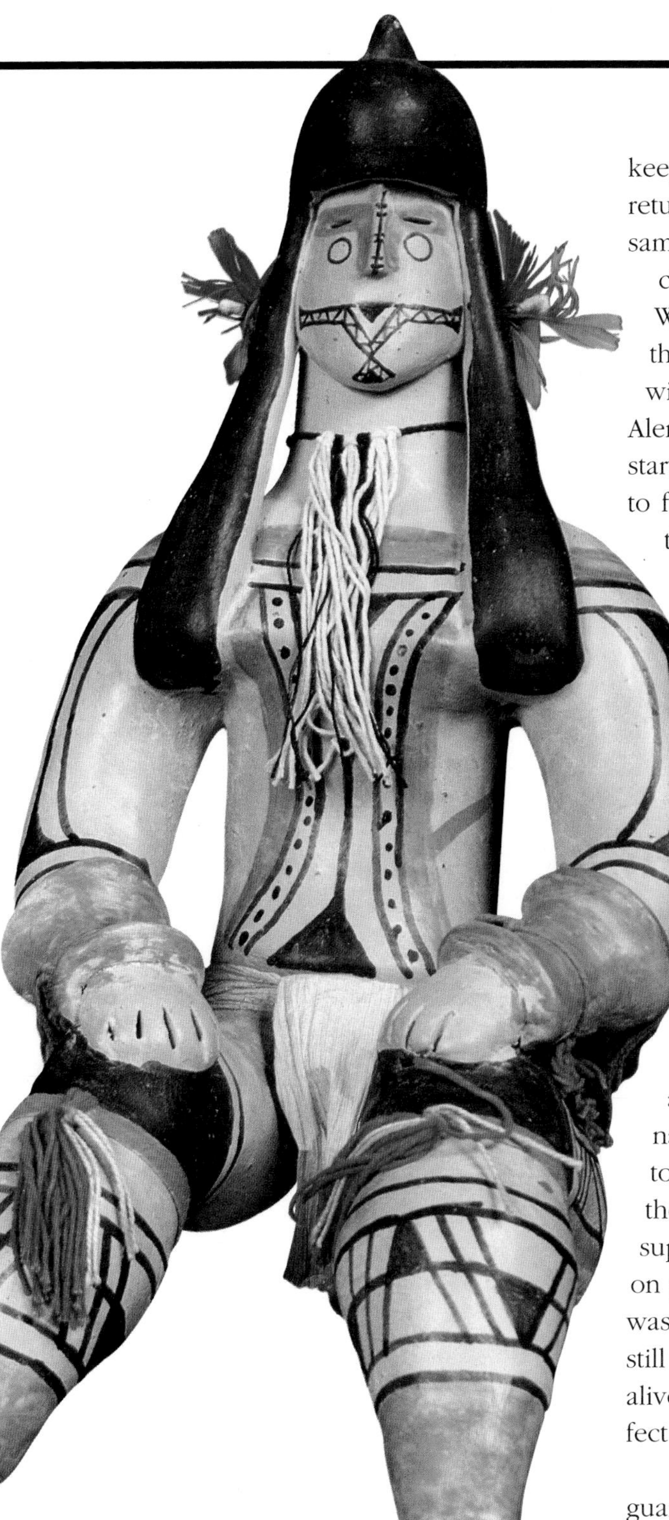

The next day the sparrow hawk stayed to keep watch over the food and, when they returned once more, the women tried to play the same trick on him. But he was not fooled and chased them back up the cord into the sky. When they were halfway up he threw a stick that broke the cord, and the women fell down with such force that they sank into the earth. Alerted by the noise, the hunters ran up and started digging up wives for themselves. The first to find the women took two or more away with them, which is why some men have several wives even today.

The Victory of Men

Another popular set of tales concerns a race of women who once held knowledge and power, until men snatched it away from them. The Tupi of the Brazilian Amazon say that once the world was ruled by women, to the growing frustration of the sun who wanted a perfect wife but found all the females on Earth too domineering for him. He hatched a plot to reverse the social order, and began by making the cucara tree impregnate a virgin called Ceucy. Her son, Jurupari, took power away from the women. He taught the men to hold regular feasts celebrating their supremacy, from which the women were banned on pain of death. The first victim of this new rule was Jurupari's own mother, Ceucy. The feasts are still held today, and the Tupi say that Jurupari is alive and well, still searching the Earth for the perfect woman to marry the sun.

Symbols of masculine superiority are fiercely guarded. The Mehinaku of Alto Xingu in Brazil have sacred flutes that women are not allowed to see, under threat of death. These instruments contain the voices of spirits, and the Mehinaku explain the customs surrounding them with a story about the ancient times. Once the flutes were owned by women who at that time also possessed everything that is needed to live a civilized

fruit pods of the genipap tree. Dolls like these were always made in pairs, showing the importance that certain tribes attached to the different but complementary roles of men and women in their societies.

The Battle of the Sexes

Much of the magical power of sacred flutes, masks and ornaments lies in the violence that was supposedly used to take them from the opposite sex. These acts of primal aggression are still ritually enacted in ceremonies throughout the South American continent.

Among the Lengua of Gran Chaco, girls are initiated into womanhood when they reach adolescence. The ceremony includes young boys, dressed in masks and feathers, carrying deer-hoof rattles to represent primitive spirits of destruction. They threaten the girls with wild cries before they are driven off by mature women as part of a ritual battle of a sort which can be seen among many of the peoples of South America.

The Canelos Quichua have a riotous drinking festival which re-enacts the union of the moon and his sister. Part of the celebration involves men bringing baskets of flowers to the women, who leap on them and pour gallons of *chicha* liquor over their heads and down their throats. Later the men have to force their way into the ceremonial house, while the women continue to bombard them with alcohol. The final stage turns into a gigantic *melée,* with men and women throwing mud and *chicha* at each other. Until quite recently, the Canelos Quichua would end up in such an aggressive state that they would launch raids against their neighbours, the Jivaro.

This 16th-century lithograph by Theodor De Bry depicts an elaborate beer-making ritual. The picture illustrates the clearly defined roles played by members of both sexes. The women, in the foreground, prepare the brew and offer it to the men, who perform a ritual dance in traditional costumes.

life. They had houses, ornaments, feather headdresses, body paint and a female chief to govern them. Men, on the other hand, lived far away from the Alto Xingu, lonely, naked and without weapons, hammocks or fire.

One day they saw the women playing the sacred Kauka flutes, and decided that these were the instruments of their degradation. So they built bull-roarers, pieces of split or perforated wood that make a terrifying din when swung about on the end of a rope, and marched into the village, scaring the women into helplessness. The men ripped off all the women's ornaments and told them that from now on only men would be able to play the sacred flutes. From then on, Mehinaku women had to submit to men.

The Chamacoco trace all modern women to a time when men used their strength to overpower them. They tell of an era when men performed a ritual in which they wore masks and pretended to be spirits. They used their disguise to strike fear into the women. But one day a mischievous son told his mother that the masks hid only human beings. When they learned that their secret was out, the men decided to rid themselves of all the women. Only one escaped the slaughter, by disguising herself as a deer. But eventually the men felt lonely on their own, and they disliked doing women's work. Yet when they found the last woman they chased her into a tree and attacked her. In their excitement, the men ripped the woman to pieces. When they had killed her and realized what they had done, each man took a piece of her flesh home. Once there the flesh began to grow and soon every man had a new wife resembling the body part that it came from, so that men who took a piece of thigh had fat wives, and those who took fingers had lean ones.

In other myths the arrival of a woman throws the world into confusion. The Ayoreo say that one day the first woman gave birth and changed everything. The rains began to fall and rivers rose from nowhere, carving through the land and killing nearly all those who dwelt there.

Fearsome Star Maidens

Mortal women are often butchered or raped in native myths, but supernatural women get their own back. Some of the most popular horror stories from the Amazon region tell of love affairs between mortal men and irresistible maidens who descend from the stars.

A young man of the Cherentes people of Brazil once gazed up at the sky and became fascinated by the beauty of the Pleiades constellation. One star in particular caught his attention, one that he wished to carry with him in his gourd wherever he went. When he finally went to sleep that night, he dreamed of the star, and woke suddenly to find a beautiful young woman with glowing eyes standing beside him. She told him that she was the star of his dreams, and insisted that he put her in his gourd. During the days that followed he would peek inside and see her burning eyes, while at night she would emerge and let him admire her beauty. One night she enticed him into climbing a magic tree which took them both to a desolate field in the middle of Heaven. There she told him to wait while she went off to gather food. Standing alone in that austere place, he suddenly heard music. He became intrigued and followed it until at last he stumbled on a festival of corpses, dancing around so that their rotten, stinking flesh swung and fell from their skeletons. He fled in terror, with the star-maiden pursuing him, telling him to come back and accusing him of disobeying her. But the man was sick of the sky world, and clambered down the tree to the ground. As he fled he heard the star's voice telling him he would return soon. And when he got back to his village he barely had time to tell his story before falling down dead.

Heroes and Monsters

Many myths tell how the attributes of civilized life, such as fire, fishing and agriculture, were offered as gifts by ancient heroes who came to Earth disguised as humans, animals or sometimes gods.

Many South American culture heroes are brothers or twins, and while they may not always set out to benefit mankind, they invariably leave useful objects or customs behind once their adventures are done. The Makiritare twins, Iureke and Shikiemona, came from two eggs that fell to Earth after their mother, a rainbow-serpent, was shot by hunters. The eggs were saved by one of the hunters, called Kawao the toad. She was the mistress of fire, which she kept in her stomach and blew forth from time to time when she wished to cook. When her food was done, she would retrieve the flames with her tongue and swallow them again to keep her secret. Kawao used her fire to hatch the eggs but did not realize the twins would grow up wanting to avenge their mother. Soon after they hatched, they dismembered Kawao, cut the fire out of her, and served her up as a meal to her unsuspecting husband, the jaguar. But they had to hide the fire so he would not know his wife was dead. They did this by dividing it in two, and putting half in the wishu tree and half in the kumnuatte tree, which is why fire can be made by rubbing these two woods together.

Other brother-heroes, such as the sun and moon of the Paraguayan Ava-Katu-Ete, compete with each other to produce game animals, hunting bows and social laws. Sometimes a trickster has to fool the twins into fulfilling their destiny. After a terrible fire destroyed the world, the Matoco bird-twins, Icanchu and Chuna, wanted to find their birthplace but were unable to recognize it in

This wooden mask, with animal teeth and hair woven from woodbark cloth, depicts Yurupary, the spirit of the forest wind. It was worn by men of the Colombian Tukuna tribe for the *moca nova*, the initiation of young women into adulthood.

the featureless wasteland. The trickster Tokwaj, aiming to get them lost, suggested they follow their outstretched fingers and told them that when they found their fingers pointing downwards they would know they had arrived. So the bird-beings were left wandering the charred Earth, growing hungrier and hungrier. But then, one day, Icanchu chanced upon a piece of charcoal which he picked up and played like a drum. As he played, it grew into a great tree, and on every branch appeared a different species of plant.

Sometimes a culture hero is mainly a monster-slayer. The forests of South America crawl with ogres, demons and evil spirits. For the Gé of Brazil the world is especially rich in half-human ogres, including frog people, dog people, bat people, horned people and animal-headed people of all kinds. Other humanoid monsters boast extravagant attributes such as grass or bee-swarms for heads, jaguar claws or fish-teeth fingers, and wings or bamboo leaves for limbs. Blue-eyed people are considered especially loathsome, and the horror stories of the Gé abound with merciless red, white, yellow and black-skinned humans. They also tell various tales of a monster called Pointed Leg, who after stumbling into a fire carved the burned stump of his leg into a point, which he used to kill and eat people until he was himself slain by a hero.

Monstrous cannibals are such common figures in South American folklore that some peoples regard them as an everyday hazard. Cannibal myths frequently end with a culture hero killing the monster, only for animals or plants to spring from its remains.

In one Matoco myth, all the men of Pozo del Tigre village achieved the status of culture heroes for killing a *welan* – an insatiable flesh-eating evil spirit. According to the myth, the people of another small village on the Paraguay River heard a woman crying one night, and when they asked her what was wrong she said that they had killed her son, and she was going to eat their sons in revenge. She kept her promise, sneaking out of her hut each night to devour a child. When parents stayed awake to keep watch, she made herself invisible and stole their children anyway. Then they tried to kill her, but because she was a *welan* she came to life again, and carried on hunting. So the people went to hide in the hollow trunk of a bottle tree, but it became so hot in the tree that they were forced out into the open again, once more vulnerable to the evil woman. Eventually, the *welan* had eaten all the children in the unfortunate village and so, her appetite still unsatiated, she moved on to Pozo del Tigre. But there the men were cleverer. After being warned of her arrival, all the hunters of the village prepared to greet her. As soon as she came in sight they shot her full of arrows and then threw her dead body on to a huge bonfire to stop her coming back to life. Bathed in the melting fat from her body, the embers of the fire spat and leapt in all directions. And the smouldering pieces that landed in the forest turned at once into jaguars, pumas, tapirs and snakes, while those that fell into the river became piranhas, stingrays and all the other animals of the deep.

Hunting was one of the skills imparted by the culture heroes and proved indispensable to forest tribes. Deadly accurate up to a range of 50m, the blow gun was the perfect tool for hunting birds or monkeys who lived high up in the forest canopy. This quiver, which holds enough darts for a morning's hunting, is made from bark-cloth by the Maku tribe who come from Venezuela.

Peert'h of the Peccaries

Among the most important skills taught by culture heroes was how to cultivate, find or catch the tribe's staple food. An animal may teach humans how to hunt its own species, or a great hunter may even become the creature he pursues.

A Chamacoco hero once went to sleep with the rope he used for tying up game under his pillow. That night he dreamed that peccaries, a type of wild pig, were talking to him, telling him that he must stop hunting them. The dream frightened him, and at first he obeyed the peccaries. Eventually, though, his fear subsided, and one day he went out hunting again, only to find himself attacked by a great herd of peccaries. He took refuge in a tree, where he stayed all day, shouting and screaming at the animals below. At last a peccary implored him to come down, assuring him he would be safe. Realizing he would starve if he stayed in the tree, the man at last decided to descend. The peccaries kept their word and did not harm him and so he joined their herd. With his knowledge of the forest, he even became their leader, but whenever he saw humans he would wave his arms, showing them how best to stalk and surround the peccaries.

The humans called him Peert'h, which means "one who is greater than a peccary". Although he helped the humans catch many pigs, they still mistrusted him, wondering if one day he would lead them into a trap where they would be eaten by their own quarry. So one day they kidnapped him and took him back to the village, intending to make him live among men so he could teach them all he knew about the ways of the forest. But he had already lived so long among the peccaries that stiff hair had grown all over his body and he had assumed the bestial ways of the wild. He no longer felt comfortable living among humans and as soon as he could, he escaped back into the safety of the forest and the company of animals.

Now he is chief of the peccaries, and although hunters often see him, he never hurts them, and instead leaves his followers and goes into hiding while the hunt is in progress.

The Taking of Fire

In a number of myths, fire marks the birth of civilization. It may come as a blaze which destroys dangerous creatures, or a gift that allows people to eat cooked food and frighten off animals.

The Opaye of the upper reaches of the Paraguay claim that the jaguar's mother was the first keeper of fire. One by one the animals tried to take it from her.

First came the armadillo, who tickled the jaguar's feet with a feather until she fell asleep, and then stole a burning brand. But as soon as the tickling stopped the jaguar woke up and called to her son, who chased the armadillo and took back the smouldering ember.

The tapir tried next, by boring the mother to sleep with his conversation, but as he tiptoed out with a burning twig in his mouth he tripped over a root and crashed to the ground, waking the jaguar's mother who at once reclaimed his prize.

One by one all the animals tried, and while most of them succeeded in getting the jaguar mother to fall asleep, none of them managed to escape with the secret of fire.

Eventually only the *prea,* a kind of guinea-pig, was left to try his luck. Instead of sending the jaguar mother off to sleep, he simply walked in and told her he wanted some fire. Then he trotted off with it. For a few moments the jaguar mother was too astonished to shout, and so the *prea* got a head start and eventually escaped. On his way home he met some humans who were fascinated by his new possession. So he gave the fire to them.

Although the jaguar no longer has fire, and is now condemned to eat his food raw, the distant memory of the flame can still be seen burning in his eyes.

Why Some People Are Warriors

Some tribes see themselves as natural fighters, declaring others their natural victims. Such peoples use their origin myths to explain their characteristics, with combat forming an important part of their rituals.

According to the Kaduveo, the creator spirit made all the races of humanity one at a time, giving each its different gifts. Some were skilled in magic, some had intelligence or strength, and others were great hunters or farmers. The Kaduveo were made last of all, and when their turn came there were no more gifts left to distribute, so the tribe was given the right to make war on all the other peoples, and steal their food, wives and children.

The Yanomami of Venezuela, who call themselves "the fierce people", practise a complicated system of ritual violence between their various groups and clans. They also explain their warlike natures with an origin myth. They claim that the first men were created after a cosmic flood, when a creature shot an arrow into the spirit of the moon, spattering its blood on to the Earth. A race of male warriors rose up from the moon spirit's blood, who were so fierce that they immediately started to exterminate each other. These angry men were called the Kanbaroma.

At this time there were no women. On rare occasions, the men stopped fighting among themselves and tried to produce heirs by rubbing themselves against each other's calf muscles. In this way the legs of Kanbaroma became pregnant. The left leg gave birth to women, and the right to men who were less aggressive than the moon-blood people. The new humans multiplied quickly and soon produced all the races of the Earth. But there were still enough of the old, fierce warriors left to mate with some of the women. Thus a new, fighting race was born, for the offspring of these liaisons became the warlike Yanomami.

The Warao, who currently live in the Orinoco delta, believe that they originated further upriver and fled downstream from a more aggressive tribe. One of their myths describes how, after descending from the skies into this arid world, they were given a lake of pure water by the supreme spirit. However, to test the people, the spirit ordered them not to bathe in the lake (the Warao are despised by neighbouring societies for their lack of hygiene). A family of four brothers and two sisters lived at the water's side, and although the brothers obeyed the law, the sisters ignored it and often went swimming.

Eventually one of the sisters, who was called Korobona, swam to the centre of the lake, where she found a pole standing upright out of the water. She was curious so she touched it, and suddenly the spirit of the lake, which had been bound to the pole, snatched her and dragged her to his underwater home. She returned home pregnant, and when the baby was born it was so handsome that, in her pride, she went to visit the lake demon again and for the second time she went home pregnant. This time, however, she bore a child that was half serpent, so her brothers killed it with their arrows. Korobona took the dead child into the forest, where she nursed it back to life, but her brothers found it again, and this time when they killed it they cut it into pieces.

Korobona collected the body together and buried it, covering it with leaf mould and various plants. She guarded the grave for some time until it spewed forth a mighty warrior, bright red and already armed for battle. This was the first of the Carib, who then proceeded to drive the Warao out of their traditional hunting grounds. This story is mirrored in at least one Carib myth which says that the Carib descended from a paradise in the sky in order to cleanse the dirty and disordered world that lay below.

Honouring the Dead

Headhunting and cannibalism are both ways of taking over another person's soul, and thus play an important part in the funeral rites of some warrior societies.

The Guayakí of Paraguay treat the bodies of their own dead as enemies, which must be eaten by the tribe. The body provides a focus for the dead person's spirit – which is potentially dangerous – and only by consuming the flesh can the spirit be dispatched into the next world. By contrast, the Tupinamba, before they ate the bodies of dead enemies, adopted them into the tribe, offering them wives, showering them with kindness and almost treating them as pets. Eating them was simply the final stage in absorbing them and making them wholly Tupinamba.

When a relative dies, the warriors of a Jivaro family make elaborate ritual preparations for a head-hunt. The trophy head, or *tzantza*, that is chosen is deboned, sewn together and shrunk. This process seals in the *muisak* soul, a part of the human spirit which, if left free, has the job of taking revenge for its owner's death.

Wearing this mask representing a trophy head, a Tapirape shaman embodied the spirits of the dead in a ritual at the onset of the dry season.

Shadows, Spirits and Shamans

Some South American Indians believe they have multiple souls. One might be the soul of their name, and govern how they act. Another would be like a shadow, shaped by the memories and thoughts of its owner. In a world filled with dangers, however, these souls become prey to evil forces and it is the shaman's task to keep such spirits at bay.

Human souls are alternatively threatened or helped by an army of spirits that inhabit the natural world. The Bororo, for example, know that they can harm a man's soul with the careful use of certain plants whose hidden souls are actually those of carnivorous animals. The soul may be driven from the body by illness or perversion; it may wander off, seduced by an attractive animal spirit; or it may be cast out by another invading soul.

Shamans are important in South American societies because they have access to the spirit world and can negotiate with its denizens. The first shamanic beings were usually gods, culture heroes or other supernatural entities. The Tukano believe that the creator, Yepá Huaké, made the first people by breathing life into them. At first he wanted them to live forever and guided them to the waters of immortality, but his unruly creations refused to bathe there, and their disobedience caused death to come into the world. In order to console the people, Yepá Huaké made the first three shamans, Payé, Yai and Kumu. These shamans provide role-models for aspiring shamans even today.

The Avá-Chiripá of Costa Rica believe that the creator, Nanderu Guazu, gave his clothes, along with his powers, to his son, the culture hero Kuarahy. The most powerful Avá-Chiripá shamans still dress in a similar way, with a gourd rattle, a breast-sash, a bracelet decorated with feathers, a feathered tiara and a feathered cross.

In Brazil, the apprenticeship of a young Kraho shaman involves re-enacting the myth of Tir'kre, who fell sick in his sleep one day because a poisonous ant crawled into his ear. Fearing the illness would bring bad luck, the rest of his people abandoned him far away from their village and he barely survived in his isolation until some vultures persuaded a cloud of humming birds to pick the ant out of his ear and carry him up to Heaven. There Tir'kre was fed raw game birds by an attentive hawk, but every time he ate one he vomited blood. While in Heaven, Tir'kre learned to change himself into an otter, an ant and various birds, before returning to Earth in the shape of a sambaiba leaf, which in skilled hands can be used either as a medicine or a poison. Sometimes when a Kraho man or woman is sick, and is quarantined from the rest of the community, he or she will be visited by either a spirit, an animal, a human, or a plant. This vision-creature heals the sick individual, feeding him or

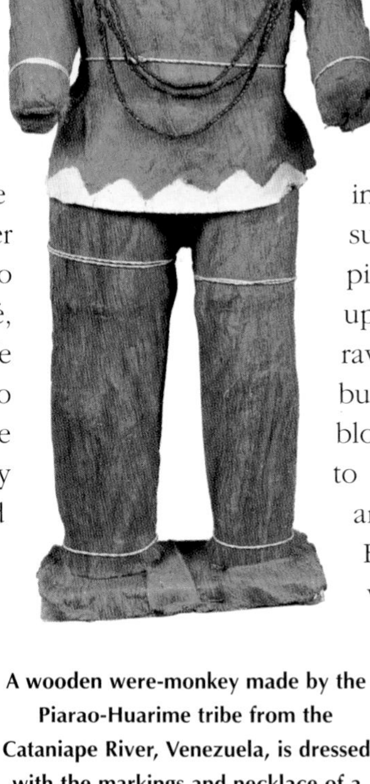

A wooden were-monkey made by the Piarao-Huarime tribe from the Cataniape River, Venezuela, is dressed with the markings and necklace of a shaman. He is fashioned from forest materials including wax, wood and cloth woven from wood bark. The red and black dyes come from the urucu and genipap trees.

her raw birds and removing poisoned fluids from the patient's body. Then the spirit helper inserts magic powers and devices directly into the newly initiated shaman, who starts by practising his or her skills in isolation before rejoining the community.

Unearthly Gifts

The powers of a shaman are not restricted to healing. Depending on the tribe, he may be able to control the weather, find fish, control the souls of the dead or bargain with the spirit rulers of all the animals for a good supply of game. Some shamans even marry the spirits of animals to ensure there is always good hunting for their peoples.

But shamans are not always benign. In many South American languages, the words for shaman and jaguar are almost the same, and the one may turn into the other by singing, reciting spells, wearing jaguar-decorations or taking hallucinogenic drugs. The Desana shaman, for example, becomes a jaguar by taking a huge dose of snuff. While his body lies sick and dizzy in a hammock, his soul prowls the jungle, eating his enemies. Even ordinary jaguars are said to be more aggressive when in the presence of a shamanic were-jaguar.

Other shamans may specialize in possessing the bodies of their victims, or shooting tiny magic darts that slowly destroy the soul of an enemy. The Warao blame all death on a dark shaman, who kills people with arrows before carrying them, upside down, to the Underworld. However, this is not necessarily a bad thing, say the Warao. Before the coming of the dark shaman, things were even worse, because people used to be under constant threat from mysterious and terrible vampires that drained the blood from the hearts of the living and carried it away to be drunk by the dark spirits of the Underworld.

This mantle was worn by a shaman during the Jivaro tribe's preparation of the *tzantza,* the shrunken head. The Jivaro, from Ecuador's Morona River, revered the toucan, whose body and feathers adorn much of their ritual clothing. They were one of the few Amazonian tribes to indulge in human sacrifice.

JOURNEY OF THE SHAMAN

Brought across the Bering Straits with the earliest immigrants to the Americas, shamanism is practised by native people from Tierra del Fuego in the south to the Arctic Circle in the north. A shaman's role in all these cultures is a combination of doctor, priest, social worker and therapist. Sometimes people turn to a shaman when they believe they are in some way cursed by the gods – for example by illness or the failure of a relationship – or when they need the future foretold. The shaman also leads important ceremonies such as initiation rituals.

A shaman does his job by entering the spirit world and interacting with the supernatural. The ability to remain in control during these encounters is what makes him special in the eyes of the tribe. He may seek out the god or demon who is causing an illness, or he may go to the gods for advice if the tribe is planning a hunt. Methods of entering the spirit world differ. Many shamans rely on chanting and dancing to induce a trance. But what distinguishes South American shamans is their ritualized use of hallucinogenic drugs. About one hundred different plants are used as hallucinogens, including datura and peyote.

Mastery of the spirit world may be lost, however, if a shaman breaks a taboo and becomes contaminated, or if he loses a power struggle with another shaman.

Bolivian shaman

Above: **A Yanomami man takes hallucinogenic snuff through a tube. In South America, hallucinogens are an essential ingredient in any shamanic soul-flight – when a person's spirit leaves the body and travels through the world of ghosts and gods.**

Right: **Costumes are an important part of some shamanic rituals. This full body costume decorated with feathers is called an *orok* and comes from the Wayana-Aparai tribe in the Amazon. The *orok* is worn during initiation ceremonies.**

Above: This textile from Paracas in Peru is decorated with flying shamans. The Paracas culture flourished from 700BC to AD200.

Right: The Moche recorded every aspect of their lives in their pottery. Here a shaman prepares coca with a wooden stick. He dates from around AD450–550.

THE AMERINDIAN LEGACY

The consequences of the European takeover were disastrous for South America's native peoples. Their wealth was plundered, their political and social structure destroyed and their gods thrown down. Yet they survived with their languages for the most part intact, and their ancient heritage, long suppressed, has never been entirely forgotten.

The destruction was at its worst in the short-lived conquistador era, when the Indian population bore the brunt both of the conquerors' greed and of the civil wars that rent their conflicting factions. Many atrocities were committed; there were reports of men being tracked down with hunting dogs and nursing mothers shot for target practice. Equally harmful in the long run was the sheer waste of economic resources; according to one governor of Cuzco, more llamas were killed in four years by the Spanish, who regarded the animals' brains and bone marrow as delicacies, than in the previous four hundred years. Meanwhile the carefully maintained terraces that had made agriculture possible on steep hillsides were allowed to crumble and irrigation channels ran dry. Built for pedestrian use, the marvellous Inca roads broke up under the hooves of Spanish horses.

Seeing their world collapsing around them, the native peoples fell into despair. The birth rate plummeted, while diseases such as measles and smallpox, to which the Indians had no immunity, took a terrible toll. Philip II of Spain wrote to the Archbishop of Lima: "We have been informed ... that many Indians hang themselves, others allow themselves to die by not eating, others take poisonous herbs, and mothers kill their babies at birth, saying that they do it to free them from the hardships they themselves suffer." The result was a cataclysmic decline in the population of the Inca lands, from possibly 7 million to 1.8 million in the forty years after Pizarro arrived. The situation was similar in Portuguese Brazil, where numbers were reduced by two thirds in less than a century.

In theory at least, the situation improved after 1542, when the Spanish monarchy took direct control. Three viceroyalties were set up: Rio de la Plata, covering what is now Argentina, Paraguay, Uruguay and Bolivia; Peru, administering that country and the northern half of Chile; and New Granada, incorporating Ecuador, Colombia and Venezuela, along with part of Panama.

The terraces on the Andes are hundreds of years old. Their maintenance was crucial to pre-Columbian civilizations. When the Spanish conquered the region, the terraces fell into disrepair, leaving the population starving.

European explorers of the 19th century had many tales to tell; this engraving by Franz Keller purports to show local huntsmen trapping the fearsome black cayman.

Under colonial rule, Amerindians never lacked influential advocates. A succession of high-minded individuals, many of them churchmen, took up their cause, and their arguments were usually well received in Madrid. Native South Americans inhabiting Spanish-owned land were, in theory at least, free citizens of Spain, and laws were passed to ensure that they were moderately taxed and were not employed as forced labour.

On the ground in America, however, much of the legislation proved a dead letter. It was accepted that the Amerindians should pay a share of local produce and of the land's mineral wealth to its new owners. In practice many were forced to work under inhuman conditions in the gold and silver mines on which Spain came to rely for much of its wealth. Others were taken from the highlands to work in coca plantations in the steamy heat of the rainforest, where they succumbed in their thousands to unfamiliar tropical diseases.

Before long a rigid class system developed. Newly-arrived settlers from the Iberian peninsula – the *peninsulares* – formed its summit. Below them came the creoles – people of Spanish or Portuguese descent who had been born in South America – and then *mestizos* of mixed European and Indian parentage. The Amerindians were at the bottom of the heap, treated as second- or third-class citizens in the lands they once ruled.

Even when revolution finally came to Spanish America in the early nineteenth century, it brought little relief. Despite the good intentions of the leading reformers, the Amerindians ended up bearing the brunt of the fighting, plundered and exploited by all sides. And when the war ended, they emerged to find their position little changed.

Throughout the Andes, the Indians' situation actually worsened under the republics that replaced the colonial regime. The Araucanians of Chile were finally subjugated in the latter half of the century, as were the native peoples of Argentina's southern and western frontiers.

Yet the nineteenth century also saw the first stirrings of an intellectual revolution that was ultimately to work in favour of the continent's indigenous peoples. First the Romantics – most of them far away in Europe – took to idealizing native peoples as "Noble Savages" – viewed as innocent and unspoiled by the evil and corrupting influence of "civilization". More realistically, knowledge of the great achievements of the Inca empire was spread by William H. Prescott's *History of the Conquest of Peru*, a classic that has remained in print continuously for the past 150 years.

Accounts such as Prescott's sparked fresh interest in relics of the lost civilization. A breakthrough was made by the American explorer Hiram Bingham, who in 1911 followed a newly-blasted road into the Urubamba valley and found the weed-choked remains of the mountain-top citadel of Machu Picchu, now one of the most visited archaeological sites in the Western world. Contemporaneously with Bingham, the German archaeologist Max Uhle was conducting a series of digs that paved the way for the first scholarly chronology of Peru's other ancient cultures.

The 1920s saw a worldwide upsurge of interest in the arts of native peoples, stimulated in part by the European avant-garde. The movement had repercussions throughout South America. Many anthropologists travelled to the continent in order to study local crafts and record myths. During this period, Brazilian composer Hector Villa-Lobos borrowed exotic percussion instruments and insistent rhythms from Amazon Indians to add a distinctive note to compositions in which he sought to capture "the sound of the jungle at night".

Henri Rousseau's fantastical *Jaguar Attacking a Horse*, painted in 1910, was inspired by tales of the rainforest from South America.

Many ancient festivals and rites are still practised in South America; here at Sacsahuayman in Peru, dancers celebrate Inti Raymi, the famous Inca festival of the sun. Today, however, tourists make up a large percentage of the audience.

The new curiosity strayed over into popular culture. Lurid travellers' tales inspired stories of the "Green Hell" of the Amazon and fuelled the fancies of such faraway observers as Henri Rousseau, a French customs inspector turned painter who never went further west than the Channel yet painted dreamlike visions of a rainforest of the imagination. The Argentine-born writer W.H. Hudson set his romance, *Green Mansions*, in the Venezuelan jungle, while Sherlock Holmes's creator Sir Arthur Conan Doyle chose the Roraima Plateau as the setting for *The Lost World*, in which dinosaurs inhabit an unexplored region on the borders of Brazil and Venezuela. More recently, the exotic appeal of the Incas has fed through into such works as Peter Shaffer's 1960s stage hit *The Royal Hunt of the Sun,* as well as films such as Roland Joffe's *The Mission* and Werner Herzog's epic *Aguirre, Wrath of God,* starring Klaus Kinski.

The appetite for such fictions had been stimulated by the real-life mystery surrounding the disappearance of the British explorer Colonel Percy Fawcett in 1925. In search of a legendary lost city, the Colonel set off in a blaze of publicity with his son and one other companion on an expedition into the jungles of the Mato Grosso region of southwest Brazil. None of the three was ever to be seen again.

Indigenous inhabitants are now facing new challenges. In the Andes their numbers have increased; perhaps 13 million live in the Inca lands today. The majority still speak Quechua, their ancestral language, and keep alive the memory of past glories. The situation is very different in the rainforest, where the Indians' very survival is under threat. Their lands have been invaded by hundreds of thousands of outsiders, attracted by a series of grandiose, government-backed development projects. The influx, already responsible for vast losses, risks upsetting the delicate ecological balance maintained by indigenous peoples over many millennia, not to mention the possible destruction of plant species used for medicines.

Nevertheless the situation is not entirely bleak. Indigenous groups in Ecuador, Colombia, Bolivia and Chile have made concrete political gains. The Indian political party in Ecuador (CONAIE) is a serious powerbroker. In Bolivia an Aymara was elected Vice President in 1993 and there is now an official policy of bilingual education. In Chile, the Mapuche have had some success in regaining land stolen from them during the Pinochet regime. Finally, in Colombia indigenous rights are now recognized in the new constitution. Although the future may not be rosy, progress is certainly being made.

Index

Page numbers in *italic* denote captions. Where there is a textual reference to the topic on the same page as a caption, italics have not been used.

Further Reading

Albisetti, Cesar (et al.) *Folk Literature of the Bororo Indians.* UCLA Latin American Center Publications, Los Angeles, 1983.
Alexander, H.B. *Latin American Mythology.* Cooper Square Publishers, New York, 1932.
Bawden, Garth *The Andean Heritage: Masterpieces of Peruvian Art from the Collection of the Peabody Museum.* Peabody Museum Press, Cambridge, Mass., 1982.
Burrin, Kathleen (ed.) *The Spirit of Ancient Peru.* Thames & Hudson, New York, 1997.
Cobo, Bernabé *History of the Inca Empire: An Account of the Indians' Customs and their Origin, together with a Treatise on Inca Legends, History and Social Institutions.* University of California Press, Austin, 1979.
Coe, Michael, Dean Snow and Elizabeth Benson *Atlas of Ancient America.* Facts on File Ltd, Oxford, 1993.
Fagan, Brian M. *Kingdoms of Gold, Kingdoms of Jade.* Thames & Hudson, London, 1991.
Hemming, John *The Conquest of the Incas.* Macmillan, London, 1970.
Lizot, Jacque *Tales of the Yanomami.* Cambridge University Press, Cambridge, England, 1991.
MacCormack, Sabine *Religion in the Andes: Vision and Imagination in Early Colonial Peru.* Princeton University Press, Princeton, 1991.
Markham, Clements *The Incas of Peru.* Smith, Elder and Co., London, 1910.
Morrison, Tony *The Mystery of the Nasca Lines.* Nonsuch Expeditions Ltd, Woodbridge, 1987.
— *The New Larousse Encyclopedia of Mythology.* Hamlyn, London, 1983.
Osborne, Harold *South American Mythology.* Newnes, Feltham, 1990.
Parks, Donald (ed.) *Myths and Traditions of the Arikara Indians.* University of Nebraska Press, Lincoln, 1996.
Steward, J.H. *Handbook of South American Indians.* (7 vols) Smithsonian Institution Bureau of American Ethnology, Washington, 1946–59.
Stierlin, Henri *Art of the Incas and its Origins.* Rizzoli, New York, 1984.
The First Voyage Around the World by Magellan 1518–1521. (translated from accounts of Pigafetta and other contemporary writers by Lord Stanley of Alderley, London, 1874).
Wachtel, N. *The Vision of the Vanquished, the Spanish Conquest of Peru through Indian Eyes, 1530–1570.* (translated by Ben and Siân Reynolds), Harvester Press, Hassocks, 1977.

Picture Credits

The Publisher wishes to thank the following people and organizations for permission to reproduce their material. Every care has been taken to trace copyright holders. If there are any omissions or errors, corrections can be made to future editions.

Key:
a above; **b** below; **c** centre; **l** left; **r** right

Abbreviations:
BM British Museum, London
ETA e.t. archive
EZS E.Z. Smith
JBT John Bigelow Taylor of New York
MARLH Museo Arquelogico Rafael Larco Herrera, Lima, Peru
MFV Museum für Volkerkunde, Berlin
SAP South American Pictures
WFA Werner Forman Archive

Title page: MARLH; **Contents page**: SAP; **6** BM; **7** BM; **10–11** SAP; **12l** WFA; **12r** SAP; **13l** ETA/Archaeological Museum of Lima; **13r** BM; **14** WFA/MFV, Berlin; **15** WFA/MFV; **16** Wolfgang Schuler; **17** JBT; **18** JBT; **19** WFA/MFV; **20–21** ETA/Naval Museum, Genoa; **22** SAP; **23** EZS; **24c** SAP; **24b** MARLH; **24–25** WFA; **25tl** MARLH; **25tr** ETA/Archaeological Museum, Lima; **26** John Cleare Mountain Camera; **27** WFA; **28** BM; **29** SAP; **30** Musée de l'Homme, Paris; **31** WFA/BM; **34** ETA/Archaeological Museum, Lima; **35** SAP; **37** WFA/MFV; **38** WFA/MFV; **39** SAP; **40–41** JBT; **42** MARLH; **43** SAP; **44** Johann Reinhard; **45** ETA/Archaeological Museum, Lima; **46** MARLH; **48** Andes Press Agency/Marcel Reyes-Cortez; **50tl** WFA; **50bl** ETA/Archaeological Museum, Lima; **50–51** ETA/Archaeological Museum, Lima; **51t** AKG, London/Erich Lessing; **51b** MARLH; **52** ETA/University Museum, Cuzco; **53** WFA/MFV; **54** SAP; **55** Johann Reinhard; **56** JBT; **58** WFA/MFV; **59** ETA/Arteaga College, Peru; **60** WFA/MFV; **61** ETA/Archaeological Museum, Lima; **62** Andes Press Agency/ Carolyn Kerson; **64** SAP; **65** SAP; **68** SAP; **69** JBT; **71** WFA/Nick Saunders/Barbara Heller; **72** JBT; **73** WFA/Museum of the American Indian, New York; **75** WFA/MFV; **76** ETA/University Museum, Cuzco; **77** SAP; **78tl** SAP; **78b** Johann Reinhard; **79tl** SAP; **79tr** SAP; **79b** SAP; **80** Dagli Orti; **81** Royal Geographical Society/Eric Lawrie; **83** John Cleare Mountain Camera; **86** Dagli Orti; **87** British Library; **89** EZS; **90** ETA/New York Public Library, New York; **91** JBT; **93** SAP; **94** Johann Reinhard; **95** Mary Evans Picture Library; **96** SAP; **97** SAP; **98** Loren McIntyre; **99** WFA; **100** Bridgeman Art Library; **101** SAP; **102l** National Geographic Society Image Collection/Bill Ballenberg; **102b** WFA/MFV; **102–103** National Geographic Society Image Collection/Nathan Benn; **103tr** Johann Reinhard; **103b** WFA/MFV; **104** SAP; **105** JBT; **106** Frank Lane Picture Agency; **107** EZS; **109** EZS; **110** EZS; **111** EZS; **112** EZS; **114** Chris Caldicott/Royal Geographical Society, London; **115** EZS; **116** EZS; **117** EZS; **118** Bruce Coleman Images; **120** EZS; **121** EZS; **122** Jean-Loup Charmet; **124–125** EZS; **126** EZS; **129** EZS; **130** EZS; **131** EZS; **132bl** SAP; **132tr** SAP; **132br** EZS; **133t** The Art Institute of Chicago; **133b** ETA/Archaeological Museum, Lima; **134** SAP; **135** SAP; **136** Bridgeman Art Library/Pushkin Museum, Moscow; **137** Andes Press Agency/John Curtis